Transform Your Space Into a Serene Bird Sanctuary

Orson .I Frame

All rights reserved. Copyright © 2023 Orson .I Frame

<u>Funny helpful tips:</u>

Prioritize quality time together; shared experiences deepen the bond.

Set clear fitness goals; having a defined target provides motivation and a clear direction for your training.

Transform Your Space Into a Serene Bird Sanctuary : Create a Whispering Haven: Unlock the Secrets to a Tranquil Avian Paradise in Your Home

Life advices:

Invest in continuous learning; the world is ever-changing, and so should your knowledge base.

Learn to apologize sincerely; taking responsibility strengthens trust.

Introduction

This is a comprehensive manual designed to help novice bird enthusiasts transform their backyards into thriving bird sanctuaries.

The guide begins by detailing various strategies on how to attract birds to your yard, emphasizing the importance of providing an assortment of foods. It delves into the types of bird-friendly foods available and offers insights into selecting the most suitable options. Additionally, it discusses the different types of feeders and how to choose the best ones, providing tips on feeder placement, predator protection, and pest-proofing.

Maintenance is another key aspect, with sections on keeping feeders and water sources clean and in good working order. The guide also addresses the significance of providing shelter and nesting opportunities for birds, touching on bird nesting box maintenance and essential terminology for bird enthusiasts.

The guide culminates in a section dedicated to various bird species, offering information about the types of birds that may visit your sanctuary and providing insights into their behavior and habits.

In essence, this book equips beginners with the knowledge and tools needed to create a welcoming and sustainable environment for wild birds in their own backyards.

Contents

How to Attract Birds to Your Yard 1
    Types of Food 2
    Choosing the Best Foods 7
    Types of Feeders 8
    Choosing the Best Feeders 20
    Feeder Placement 20
    Protection from Predators 21
    Pest-Proofing Your Feeders 22
    Feeder Cleaning and Maintenance 23
    Water Sources 23
    Placement of Water 25
    Water Source Cleaning and Maintenance 25
    Shelter and Nesting 25
    Bird Nesting Box Maintenance 27
    Helpful Terms to Know 27

The Birds 30
American Crow 31
American Goldfinch 33
American Robin 35
American Tree Sparrow 37
Baltimore Oriole 39
Bewick's Wren 42
Black-capped Chickadee 44
Black-chinned Hummingbird 46

Blue Jay	48
Brown-headed Cowbird	50
Brown Thrasher	52
Bushtit	54
Carolina Wren	56
Chipping Sparrow	60
Common Grackle	64
Dark-eyed Junco	66
Downy Woodpecker	68
Eastern Bluebird	72
Eastern Phoebe	74
Eurasian Collared-Dove	78
European Starling	80
Fox Sparrow	82
Gray Catbird	84
Hairy Woodpecker	88
House Finch	92
House Sparrow	94
House Wren	96
Lesser Goldfinch	100
Mourning Dove	102
Northern Cardinal	104
Northern Flicker	106
Northern Mockingbird	108
Pileated Woodpecker	110
Pine Siskin	114
Pine Warbler	118

Purple Finch 120

Purple Martin 122

Red-bellied Woodpecker 124

Red-breasted Nuthatch 128

Red-winged Blackbird 132

Rose-breasted Grosbeak 134

Ruby-throated Hummingbird 136

Song Sparrow 140

Spotted Towhee 142

Tufted Titmouse 146

Varied Thrush 149

White-breasted Nuthatch 151

White-crowned Sparrow 155

White-throated Sparrow 157

Yellow-rumped Warbler 159

PART 1

How to Attract Birds to Your Yard

Attracting birds to your yard will take a little effort and some patience, but over a weekend you can set up very basic feeding and watering components. This does not need to be an expensive venture; you can choose to repurpose items or purchase specialized feeders and baths depending on your budget. If you like, you can also attract birds by providing shelter in the form of birdhouses during the nesting months. By using the information in *The Backyard Bird Sanctuary*, you'll have the confidence to reimagine your own backyard as a haven for birds. Whatever degree of interest you have in your local feathered friends, you are sure to start a lifelong hobby in bird-watching.

Types of Food

The type of food you provide will determine which birds come to your backyard. There are ten main types of food you can purchase to place in feeders in your yard. Some of these are specific to one type of bird. Nectar, for example, is only for hummingbirds. Other types of food are eaten by a variety of birds. The types of seed you use is based on what birds you want to attract to your yard and the budget you have for feeding them. A list of each species' preferred food is provided in its entry so you can quickly determine what types of food you should have on hand for whichever type of bird you want to attract.

Sunflower

While not the most common seed in regular wild birdseed mix, sunflower seeds are one of the best because they will attract many birds. The best variety to go with is black oil sunflower seed since it has a thinner hull and supplies more calories per seed for birds. When buying sunflower seed, you have a choice between regular and hulled seed. If you don't want to have a lot of seed waste under your feeders, you can upgrade to the hulled variety. Birds do not eat the whole seed; they remove the kernel from the hull (or outside coating), which then falls to the ground.

Safflower

Safflower is similar to, but smaller than, sunflower seed and has a hull that is harder to remove. This characteristic may discourage some of the more aggressive birds, such as blackbirds and starlings, from eating it. This allows cardinals and finches to gather at the feeder and have a food they enjoy.

Cracked Corn

Another common and inexpensive food is cracked corn. This will attract many of the ground feeders in your area, such as doves, sparrows, juncos, and so on. No feeders are needed; you simply scatter the corn on the ground where you would like to attract the birds. For some smaller birds, this may be near shrubbery or a brush pile.

Nyjer Seed

Another common food is thistle, or Nyjer seed. This seed is the favorite food of the finches. The seed is very small and requires a specialized tube feeder. The feeder has a much smaller opening for the seed to be extracted from the tube. Nyjer seed is a little more expensive, but it will last longer because only the finches will be able to access and eat it.

Suet

Suet is a high-energy food source and is excellent to use during the winter months (if you have cold winters). Suet comes in many forms, including raw beef suet that you can purchase at the meat market or in cakes, which have different types of seed mixed in it. This is a favorite of woodpeckers, chickadees, and nuthatches, among others. Suet is more of a winter season food source since it gets soft or rancid in higher temperatures, unless you live at relatively high altitudes, where it is cooler. Another option is to purchase varieties of suet cakes that will not melt in higher temperatures.

Nectar or Sugar Water

A beloved visitor to backyards is the hummingbird, and their source of food is nectar. Nature provides nectar through flowers, but you can make your own nectar for hummingbirds. The typical recipe is ¼ cup granulated sugar dissolved in hot water to make 1 cup of solution. Let it cool to ambient temperature before placing the liquid in feeders. Do not add red food coloring to the liquid because of the presence of Red Dye #40, which will be ingested at rates well above comparable human safety levels. No conclusive studies have been done on this, but it would be better to err on the side of caution and refrain from using the coloring. Nectar can also be purchased premade.

Peanuts

Peanuts are another great source of energy for birds because they are high in fat. You can feed your backyard birds this food in two forms. Peanut hearts are peanuts that have been broken up. Shelled peanuts are also an option, but only the larger birds, such as Blue Jays or woodpeckers, can extract the peanut from the shell. For a cleaner yard, use shelled peanuts or put whole peanuts in mesh feeders to catch the empty shells and limit the waste that will fall to the ground.

Fruit

Fruit can be a great source of food, especially for orioles. The typical fruits to put out are oranges, apples, and melon. Some dried fruits, such as raisins, are found in seed mixes. Be mindful that some fruits (grapes and raisins) can be toxic to dogs, and refrain from using them if you or your neighbors have dogs as pets.

Jelly

Believe it or not, some birds will actually eat jelly. You should place only enough jelly in the feeder that will be consumed each day. While it might be easy to grab a jar from your pantry, be sure to use jellies made for birds, since they will have less sugar and no additives or preservatives. Some evidence suggests that birds will alter the feeding of their young and themselves because of the presence of high-fructose corn syrup in their diet. Also, feeding jelly during nesting times may cause the young to not acquire the proper nutrition from insect and seed sources.

Mealworms

Mealworms are the larvae of the darkling beetle and can be a source of food for those birds in your yard that are typically insect eaters, and will encourage even more bird species to visit. Unlike most of the other sources of food mentioned, mealworms are a great source of protein. They can be purchased roasted or raised as live larvae.

Choosing the Best Foods

While it may be the easiest way to buy birdseed, avoid bags of wild birdseed mix without first checking its contents. Mixed seed contains many types of seed (sunflower, milo, millet, corn, and others), but you will probably notice that many of the birds peck at the seed to remove the seed types they do not want. This seed falls to the ground and is then eaten by ground feeders. After you have fed the birds for a while, check the ground for seed types in quantities that suggest it is not being eaten very much or at all. If this is the case, you may want to consider changing the birdseed mix you are buying. This uneaten seed can become a source of food for pests you would rather not have in your yard. It is better to spend a little more on specific seed types and have the birds eat all of it than to watch your hard-earned money go to waste. If you do want seed mixtures, take some time and check to see what is included and in what percentages. After purchasing and placing the mix in feeders, observe the birds eating and see if they are being picky about what they are eating.

Types of Feeders

When starting to design your backyard sanctuary, it is easy to get lost in all the details of how to attract birds by feeding them. The simple solution is to know what birds you are trying to attract, find out what their preferred foods are, and then acquire the feeder for that type of bird.

Tray

One of the simplest feeders to start with in your yard is the tray feeder. You can buy one or easily make one with a piece of plywood and lengths of molding for the sides. The open platform makes it easy for every bird to land and feed, allowing for quick discovery of the feeder. While this may be nice at the beginning, you may decide later to focus on specific birds to feed and purchase other types of feeders.

Hopper

A hopper feeder is a great introductory feeder or upgrade from the tray feeder. This feeder usually has a smaller perching area and will discourage some of the larger birds from dominating the scene. Another advantage is that the seed is distributed over time from the hopper, which is under a simple roof, keeping the seed dry from inclement weather. Depending on the size of the hopper and the number of birds using the feeder, the hopper may hold food for several days.

Tube

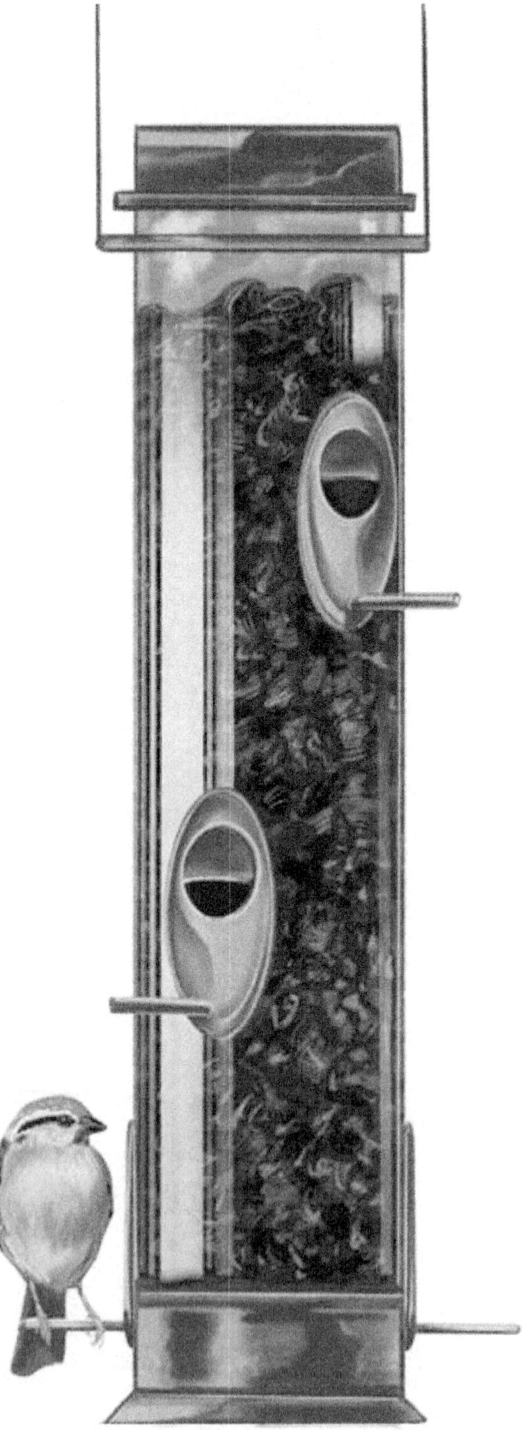

One of the most common feeders today is the tube feeder. Each opening in the tube has a small perch for birds to sit on. The typical seed to go in a tube feeder is sunflower, but it also holds mixed seed varieties just fine. Tube feeders can be purchased in different sizes, varying from perching for two birds up to six or more. Perching trays can be attached to some models. As with a tray feeder, having a large area for birds to perch on can sometimes attract the more gregarious species, like starlings and blackbirds. If you have larger, unwanted species feeding from your tube feeders, there are mesh cages that can be added to the feeder to allow only smaller birds to gain access to the seed.

Nyjer

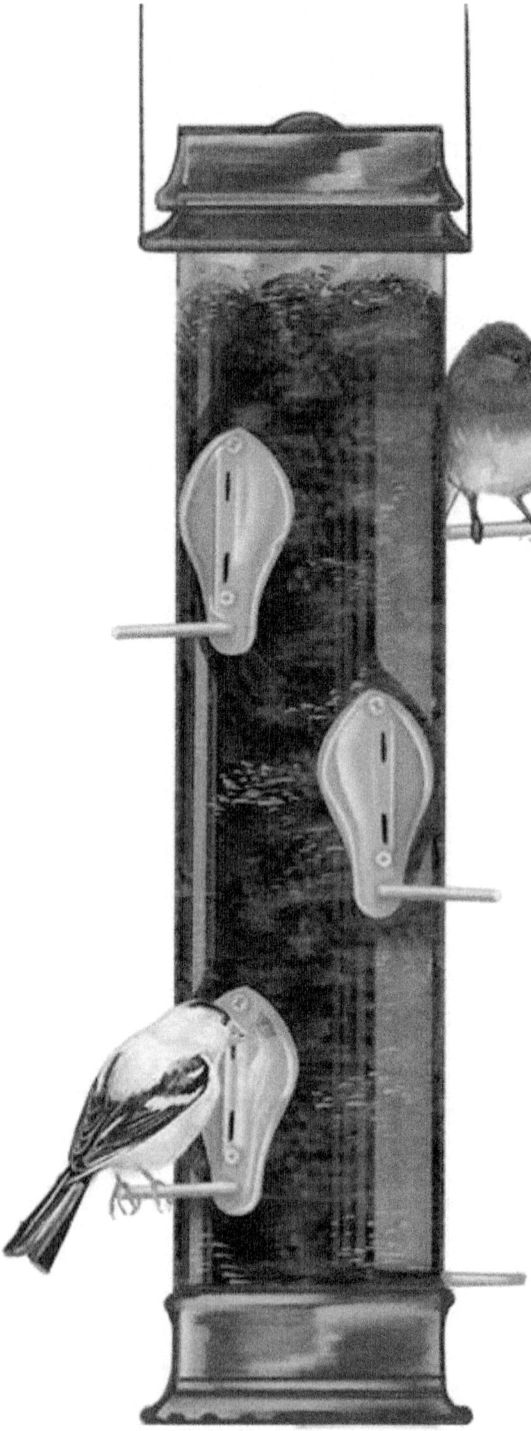

A specialized tube feeder is needed for Nyjer, or thistle, seed. It has very small openings for finches to extract the seed from the feeder. Larger birds will not be able to access the thistle seed because of the size of their bills.

Suet

If you are providing suet to your feathered friends, you need to purchase a suet feeder. A suet feeder is usually a wire-framed feeder with large mesh openings. Place either raw suet pieces or suet cakes inside for woodpeckers, nuthatches, chickadees, and other species to feed on.

Nectar

A goal for many backyard bird-watchers is to attract hummingbirds. There are two typical styles of hummingbird feeders: the flat covered saucer or the inverted glass jar, sometimes with fake red flowers. Both work equally well, so it is a matter of owner preference and daily consumption. If you are in an area with numerous hummingbirds, you can opt for either a larger-capacity feeder or several smaller feeders. Place nectar inside, but a word of caution: You will need to replace the contents with fresh nectar every few days to avoid bacterial and mold growth in the nectar solution, which can be dangerous to the hummingbirds.

Fruit and Jelly

The fruit feeder is a simple feeder; it usually has one or two bowls about the size of a typical orange. You can spoon jelly or place small pieces of fruit into these bowls. Use very small portions of jelly (spoonfuls at a time) to avoid small birds getting covered in jelly and perishing. You can also place fruit on a peg or nail on a tree trunk.

Wire Mesh

These feeders are used for multiple food sources, such as peanuts in the shell, mealworms, smaller fruit pieces or dried fruit, and seed cakes. They are available in different-sized mesh, depending on the food source you wish to place inside.

Choosing the Best Feeders

There are many different types of bird feeders, and to the beginning backyard birder they all look great. However, as you begin your search for feeders to add to your backyard, you should look for certain features. Focus your attention on function versus appearance. Some people like to have feeders that look very ornate. You want to make sure the feeder does not allow the seed to get wet and that pests can't take the seed out of the feeder. If squirrels are present in your location, the feeder you select should have metal reinforcements around the seed openings to prevent squirrels from chewing apart the plastic on tube feeders. Many feeders have squirrel-resisting features, which will be discussed in the Pest-Proofing Your Feeders section later in this part. Some feeders have bottoms that detach, making cleaning much easier. Some feeders are designed to be all-in-one, allowing mixed seed, suet, and Nyjer seed to be eaten from the same feeder. Different types of birds come to these feeders but have different behaviors. Some birds are not tolerant of a very busy feeder and may avoid your feeder for another. For example, woodpeckers will eat suet but do not like to be crowded out by the House Sparrows and starlings that come in for the mixed seed. Usually such feeders fall short of the expectations we have for them. It is better to get the style designed for the specific food you plan to provide or the bird you wish to attract.

Feeder Placement

There are many considerations to factor in when placing bird feeders in your yard. Birds can be wary of feeders placed totally in the open. A good rule to follow is to place the feeder at least 10' from any building, fence, or large plant, like trees or shrubs. This will protect the birds by allowing them to see a predator approaching. In addition, this distance will deter squirrels from gaining access to the feeder. If your yard doesn't allow for a 10' radius, you will definitely want to invest in caged-in feeders and posts with squirrel baffles to limit the seed loss due to squirrels. Be aware that any feeders placed on or near the ground are approachable by any animal that will eat the seed or food placed there. Placing seed feeders near trees, shrubs, brush piles, and such will provide a perching location for birds to approach when they are comfortable with the surrounding conditions.

Feeders can be placed on the ground, on poles, on fence posts, or hung from a tree branch. The location depends on what options you have with your yard. Since hummingbirds are attracted to nectar, placing a hummingbird feeder near flowers that they naturally visit will make it easy for them to notice a new feeder. If you have a window that is accessible, a window feeder can be a lot of fun. These are usually clear acrylic platforms that allow you to see the birds up close. This can be an exciting option for children; a feeder like this can be a first close encounter with animals, piquing their interest in nature and stewardship.

Protection from Predators

According to the American Bird Conservancy, about 2.5 billion birds are killed each year by household cats. To prevent the birds in your yard from becoming victims of felines, there are several things you can do to protect the birds. Placing feeders more than 10' away from shrubs will allow birds to see a cat approaching. Placing bells on cats' collars provides a little warning for birds to flee the area.

Many people would rather not have hawks in their backyards, but raptors are part of the food chain and may take small birds from your yard. There is no ultimate solution to this problem, but as in the case of cats, there are ways to give your feeding birds a chance to visit your feeders again. Raptors will usually scope out an area before attacking, so you should remove any obvious vantage points, such as dead limbs on trees. A brush pile can provide a bit of shelter to hide in when a hawk does visit. Birds need to be wary of other predators, but most of these issues come up when birds are nesting, and will be discussed in the Shelter and Nesting section.

Pest-Proofing Your Feeders

Hanging feeders from trees or on wooden posts provides a way for squirrels to get to a feeder. Your best option to avoid this is to place your feeders on metal poles with a squirrel baffle—a cone- or cylinder-shaped barrier—installed on those poles. This blocks squirrels or raccoons from reaching the feeder. You will want to make sure the baffle is placed at least 4' above the ground, since squirrels are known to make 4' vertical jumps and bypass the baffle. Another quick fix to squirrel pillaging is to place feeders at least 10' away from any tree, building, or structure they might use to jump onto the feeder. Feeders with cages around them can also prevent squirrels and raccoons from getting to the seed. If your feeder doesn't have a cage, make sure the feeder openings are reinforced with metal inserts. Without them, squirrels will chew on the plastic tubing, and all the seed will fall out through the hole.

Some feeders have mechanisms that close the portion where seed is released when a heavier animal is at the feeder. So, for example, a lightweight bird on the feeder can eat the seed, but a squirrel's weight will close it and prevent the squirrel from feeding.

Smaller rodents on the ground (mice, rats, etc.) can also present problems for backyard bird-watchers. To keep these critters away, make sure the seed storage area is away from the feeders. Rodents will eventually find spilled seed on the ground, but keeping your supply near feeders may enable them to find the main supply. Place any bird food in sealed containers, check periodically for damage caused by rodents, and replace damaged containers immediately. Avoid using wooden posts for holding feeders, as mice can climb them. Stop using ground platform feeders if rodents do become a problem, since it will be too easy for them to access the food. Finally, periodic cleaning of seed waste around your feeders will decrease the amount of food available to small rodents.

Deer can also become a nuisance around bird feeders. In addition to fencing in your yard, there are a few strategies you can try to keep them from eating your seed. First, clean up periodically underneath feeders so they do not have easy access to food. Second, raise feeders to at least 7' since deer can stand on their rear legs to get to feeders. Then use a hooked pole to get feeders down to refill.

For both squirrels and deer, you can buy seed that has been sprayed with hot pepper. Birds do not mind the hot pepper, but the deer and squirrels will avoid it.

The last group of pests are bees, wasps, and ants, which present problems with nectar feeders. The best way to deal with these problems depends on which type of feeder you buy. For saucer-style feeders, make sure yours has a water moat. This is a central area around the hanger hook that is filled with water so ants cannot get to the sugar water source. In hotter weather, make sure this moat is always filled with water. To discourage wasps and bees, make sure your feeder has bee guards (plastic mesh shields) that keep bees away from the openings to the sugar water. Finally, place feeders in the shade, where wasps are less likely to go. This will also prevent the nectar from becoming contaminated in the hot sun.

Feeder Cleaning and Maintenance

With use and changing weather conditions, your bird feeders need to be cleaned periodically. Bird droppings get on feeders, and rain may get inside feeders and cause the seeds inside to get moldy. Both of these conditions can be detrimental to the birds' health. The process of cleaning feeders is relatively simple and shouldn't take long. The best time to clean the feeder is when it is empty or near empty. Remove any seed and seed waste left in the feeder. You may need to use a probing tool to remove any material wedged into tight spaces that will not fall out. Using a bleach solution (10 parts water to 1 part bleach), thoroughly clean the interior and exterior surfaces. Be sure to completely rinse the feeder with water to remove any bleach solution and then let it dry out completely. Once dry, the feeder can be refilled and placed outside for use again.

For nectar feeders, make sure to clean the bee guards and water moat of any mold growth.

Water Sources

Birds need water for drinking and bathing, so the next step in creating the perfect backyard habitat for birds is to provide a source of water for them. This can be accomplished easily if you choose the simplest form—a birdbath. You can create your own with an inverted metal garbage can cover. Support it with decorative rocks underneath, and this bath will take less than an hour to create. You can also purchase a ceramic or concrete birdbath. When deciding on a container for your birdbath, there are a few things to consider for the safety of the birds. First, the water should gradually get deeper from the outside rim to the center. Second, the maximum depth should be less than 2" to avoid any small songbirds from drowning. It only takes a few seconds for a bird to become disoriented after slipping in deeper water and songbirds are poor swimmers and could perish. Third, the inner surface must have some texture for the birds to grip when standing in the bath. Small stones placed inside the bath will help keep the depth gradual while adding texture for the birds to grip. People have been successful with baths low to the ground or set on a pedestal stand. Your yard design will help you decide which is best.

One way to entice birds to your birdbath is to have movement in the water. You can do this by hanging a container that has a small hole for dripping above the birdbath. If you have access to electricity close to the birdbath, you can add a water pump, mister, bubbler, or dripper to the ground or pedestal birdbath. Another option is a solar-powered water agitator that continuously moves the water in the birdbath. If you are interested in attracting birds year-round and you live in an area with freezing temperatures, you will want to plan out your bathing stations. To keep the birdbath water from freezing, you can install an electrical heater, which means the birdbath must be near an electrical outlet. Some birdbaths have a heater integrated into the design, giving it a less cluttered look.

For those with the space and means, the ultimate water source is a backyard pond. Ponds can be made with various preformed plastic liners, or you can use plastic sheeting to design your own shape. Keep in mind the edges must be shallow for smaller birds, and rocks along the edge will help you create a gradual change in water depth. More specific information is beyond the scope of this book, but you can find books or online articles on this topic.

Placement of Water

The same considerations apply to the placement of a birdbath as to a bird feeder. It should be out of direct sunlight for the whole day. Birdbaths at ground level should be placed at least 10' from shrubs so predators such as cats can be detected by the birds in ample time to escape. To accommodate for preference by specific species, having both ground and pedestal-style birdbaths is ideal.

Water Source Cleaning and Maintenance

Do not add chemicals to the water to keep it clean or to stop the water from freezing, as this can be toxic to birds. Remember, this birdbath will also be a source of drinking water for the birds. Over time, the water will get dirty from bathing and excrement. Water left stagnant will also develop algae. The water should be changed often depending on its condition. The inner surface should be scrubbed occasionally using a bleach solution to remove any algae beginning to grow and to remove any other debris that may become a source of bacteria. Be sure to rinse the bath out completely before refilling with fresh water. Remember, in warmer temperatures, you may need to refill the bath more frequently due to the water evaporating at a faster rate.

Shelter and Nesting

While birds are in your yard, they are seeking shelter. The most common reason is to escape predation by a number of animals—mainly hawks and cats. Predators can also threaten eggs and hatchlings; raccoons, snakes, and even squirrels may raid an unprotected nest. There are a few things you can do to help adult and baby birds stay alive. Planting trees and shrubs around your yard will provide places for the birds to fly to and hide in. Instead of disposing the trimmings from trees, consider making brush piles in strategic locations, such as near ground feeders and birdbaths. Again, maintain about 10' of distance between the birdbath and the brush pile so predators will not have a place to launch their attack.

Another reason birds take shelter is seasonal nesting. Bird nests are probably one of the most identifiable things in nature. Children call out their locations when they spot one in a bush or a tree. One common misconception is that birds go back to their nests every night while they are in your location. Bird nests are only for nesting purposes: the laying of eggs and feeding of the hatchlings. Once the baby birds have fledged (are able to fly and leave the nest), they will roost elsewhere at night. Some species lay one clutch of eggs, while others will have several broods. Nesting usually occurs in mid to late spring to give the young enough time to mature and prepare for either migration in fall or for the winter season. All species make their own nests, but some build nests in man-made birdhouses or platforms. In addition, robins, phoebes, and House Sparrows, among others, will construct their nests on parts of buildings. Birds nesting in your yard will depend on the species in your area and the flora of your backyard habitat.

To encourage birds to nest in your yard, you can provide birdhouses. There are generally two types of birdhouses—the shelf and the nest box. The shelf is an open platform on which a bird will build its nest. Only a few backyard bird species will use these, but if you are interested, they are relatively easy to make. The nest box is the typical roofed birdhouse you see in magazines and in stores. It usually has a sloped roof on a constructed box with a round opening on the front. You can purchase birdhouses, or, if you are handy, you can make your own. There are a few things to keep in mind though. The interior of the birdhouse should not be painted or varnished. Birds are just looking for a place to lay their eggs, so constructing your own out of scrap wood is sufficient. Providing more expensive and overly decorative birdhouses may look very nice to us, but will not attract birds in any greater numbers than the simple ones. To help the fledglings exit the birdhouse, you may want to roughen the inside surface of the front panel to give them a place to grasp with their feet as they climb out of the birdhouse.

The best way to encourage a specific bird to nest in a house is to have the correct hole size for that species. If the hole is too large, other species will occupy the space. If it is more than 2", you have a high chance of attracting starlings and House Sparrows. The bird entries in this guide will list the size of the birdhouse and the appropriate-sized hole for each particular species, as well as the best height and location for the birdhouse. For shelf styles, the entry will list the size of the platform and how many sides to add.

For nest boxes, you will need six panels—a floor, two sides, a front panel with a hole, a roof extending past the front panel, and an oversized back panel for mounting to a tree or post. The floor panel should have its corners cut to leave small triangular openings for any water to drain out of the nest box.

One thing to consider when maintaining your property is to leave dead trees or old fence posts standing. These can provide shelter for cavity-nesting birds that will use the rotting tree or post as a nesting site. By all means, if a tree presents a danger to a house or residents, it should be removed. But if you own a larger parcel of land and can let the tree remain, those birds will thank you for your thoughtfulness.

Bird Nesting Box Maintenance

After each successful nesting in a birdhouse, it will need to be cleaned. The easiest way to do this is to construct birdhouses with a panel that can be removed or swung open in order to gain access to the inside. Some are designed with a hinged roof, while others have hinged side doors for access. When making the house, be sure to have a locking mechanism to secure this removable panel, such as a latch, screw, or pin. Once you are certain that the young birds have left the nest for good, remove the old nest and clean the interior. Scrub the inside and outside surfaces with a bleach solution to remove any avian parasites, such as bird lice or mites. Rinse thoroughly with water and let all parts dry completely before reassembling. Make sure that all locking mechanisms are still working and that all screws and nails are properly affixed. Promptly replace any birdhouses that cannot be repaired. Finally, make sure the drain holes are still of sufficient size to let water out but keep any pests from entering.

Helpful Terms to Know

As you become an experienced bird-watcher, you'll learn a lot of the words and phrases used to describe birds, their nests, and their nesting environment. Here are some of the more common ones.

baffle
A shield used to deter animals from approaching a feeder.

cache
A temporary hiding place.

fledge
When a bird is able to leave the nest.

hulled
Having the outer layer of seed removed.

migrate
To move from one region to another.

nectar
Sugary solution made by plants to attract pollinators.

nest
A structure used to lay eggs in and raise nestlings.

nestling
A young bird not yet able to leave the nest.

perch
Any object that a bird can sit on.

plumage
The overall feathering of a bird.

predation
The eating of one animal by another.

roost
The location for overnight perching.

species

A distinct kind of plant or animal.

PART 2

The Birds

Now that you know how to construct and furnish a bird-friendly backyard sanctuary, let's take a look at the wide variety of birds you can attract. Here are fifty commonly found American birds.

American Crow
Corvus brachyrhynchos

Male and female American Crows are identical in appearance.

GENERAL INFORMATION

- **Male:** A large all-black bird with a thick bill.
- **Female:** The female American Crow is not visibly different from the male.
- **Range:** All of the US except for the southwestern states.
- **Migration:** Found year-round in its range.
- **Preferred Food:** Cracked corn, peanuts, suet, sunflower seed.
- **Preferred Feeders:** Ground forager, tray feeder.
- **Nesting:**
    - **Natural:** Found in taller trees and made from branches and twigs.
    - **Man-made:** Will not nest in man-made structures.
- **Eggs:** Blue with heavy brown streaking and splotching, approximately 1 ½"–2" long.

TIPS FOR ATTRACTING

- **Provide large, deep birdbaths to accommodate the American Crow's size.**
- **Place shelled peanuts on the ground so they are visible to crows as they fly over, and they are very likely to stop in your yard to feed.**
- **Crows may gather nesting materials from backyards, such as larger twigs, and may build a nest if there are larger trees in your backyard.**

IN YOUR YARD

American Crows are your backyard birds' friends, since they sound the call when a predator, such as a cat or hawk, is nearby. Crows may form large groups when roosting in the evening, often in the hundreds. Like the Blue Jay—they're part of the same family—crows can be aggressive toward other birds and will mob hawks and owls if present. Crows are opportunistic feeders and will scavenge garbage for food. If you want to avoid having American Crows in your yard, make sure all trash is securely stored away. Crows are known to raid other birds' nests and steal the chicks for food.

American Goldfinch
Spinus tristis

Male and female

GENERAL INFORMATION

- **Male:** A small bright yellow bird with black forehead, wings, and tail.
- **Female:** The female is similar to the male but with duller yellow and less marked forehead.
- **Range:** Found in all of the US.
- **Migration:** Winters in southern third with summer migration to northern Plains states, other parts of range year-round.
- **Preferred Food:** Millet, sunflower seed, thistle seed; may take seeds from garden flowers.
- **Preferred Feeders:** Hopper feeder, thistle feeder, tray feeder, tube feeder.
- **Nesting:**
  - **Natural:** Found in hedges and border areas and made from woven plant fibers.
  - **Man-made:** Will not nest in man-made structures.

- **Eggs:** Creamy bluish with sparse brownish spots, approximately ⅝" long.

TIPS FOR ATTRACTING

- **Be sure to have Nyjer seed and sunflower seed feeders in your yard for the American Goldfinch.**
- **Maintain feeders throughout late summer since goldfinches are one of the latest-nesting songbirds, laying eggs in late July and August.**
- **Goldfinches love the seeds of zinnias, coneflowers, asters, and sunflowers, so planting these in gardens will attract them even if you do not supply them with Nyjer seed.**
- **Goldfinches like to feed in groups, so have enough feeders to accommodate the number of birds visiting.**

IN YOUR YARD

American Goldfinches eat seeds almost exclusively during the nesting season, so your feeders can become a critical source of food for nestlings. If you plan on having feeders out during the nesting time of goldfinches, maintain them until at least early fall for the young to have sufficient food. They are one of the few backyard birds that have different plumage in summer and winter. Winter males are duller and lack the black forehead, while the female is duller and more muted, with a lighter breast.

American Robin
Turdus migratorius

Male and female

GENERAL INFORMATION

- **Male:** A medium-sized bird with slate-gray back and wings, black head, and red-orange breast.
- **Female:** The female is very much like the male but with duller breast and slate-gray on the head.
- **Range:** Found throughout almost all of the US.
- **Migration:** Year-round in most of its range, winters in extreme southern parts of the US.
- **Preferred Food:** Berries, fruit, insects and worms, mealworms, suet.
- **Preferred Feeders:** Ground forager, fruit/jelly feeder, suet feeder, wire mesh (fruit, mealworms).
- **Nesting:**
  - **Natural:** A mud and grass cup, found in trees or under eaves of houses.

- **Man-made:** 7" D × 8" W × 12" H shelf style, 2 sides open, sloped roof, 6'–15' above the ground.
- **Eggs:** Unmarked sky blue, approximately 1 ¼" long.

TIPS FOR ATTRACTING

- **When placing platforms for nesting, put them in a wind-protected area away from frequent human interruptions.**
- **Robins come to freshly watered lawns or where soil has been turned over to look for insects and especially earthworms.**
- **Fall robins and returning spring robins will eat the fruit from many trees and shrubs, including holly, viburnum, grape, crab apple, dogwoods, and mulberries. Planting these varieties will attract this species during these seasons.**

IN YOUR YARD

American Robins are persistent in making their nests. Many people would like them to nest in their yards, but the location of the nests near doors can lead to a slightly messier area or unwanted dive-bombing by scared robin parents. If you can deal with this for a few weeks, you will be rewarded with seeing the young robins learning how to fend for themselves. To discourage nesting, placing a mass of wired mesh in the attempted nesting site will force the birds to go elsewhere. Young robins look like their parents but with dark spots on a whitish breast until the orange-red plumage grows in.

American Tree Sparrow
Spizelloides arborea

Male and female American Tree Sparrows are identical in appearance.

GENERAL INFORMATION

- **Male:** A small plump bird with rusty red cap, reddish-brown back, and grayish breast with a single dark spot.
- **Female:** The female American Tree Sparrow is not visibly different from the male.
- **Range:** Found in northern two-thirds of the US.
- **Migration:** American Tree Sparrows are found in the US only during winter.
- **Preferred Food:** Cracked corn, millet, peanut hearts, sunflower seed.
- **Preferred Feeders:** Ground forager, hopper feeder, tray feeder.
- **Nesting:**
    - **Natural:** Found in trees and shrubs of the tundra.
    - **Man-made:** Will not nest in man-made structures.
- **Eggs:** Blue-green with heavy splotching, approximately ⅞" long.

TIPS FOR ATTRACTING

- **Brush piles in your yard will provide shelter in winter conditions.**
- **Spread seed on the ground, or if snow is present, you may want to tamp down snow by walking on it before spreading seed so that it remains visible and accessible to the sparrows.**
- **Depending on your location and conditions, American Tree Sparrows may gather in flocks up to fifty birds. If this happens, stock up on seed so that feeding is not abruptly interrupted.**

IN YOUR YARD

American Tree Sparrows will start migrating to winter grounds in late October and will return northward in March. They are well adapted to living in cold areas and will frequent open fields and farmland for food. Deeper snow may cause them to visit feeders, and if they are present in your area during the winter, consider keeping food out for them throughout the winter.

Baltimore Oriole
Icterus galbula

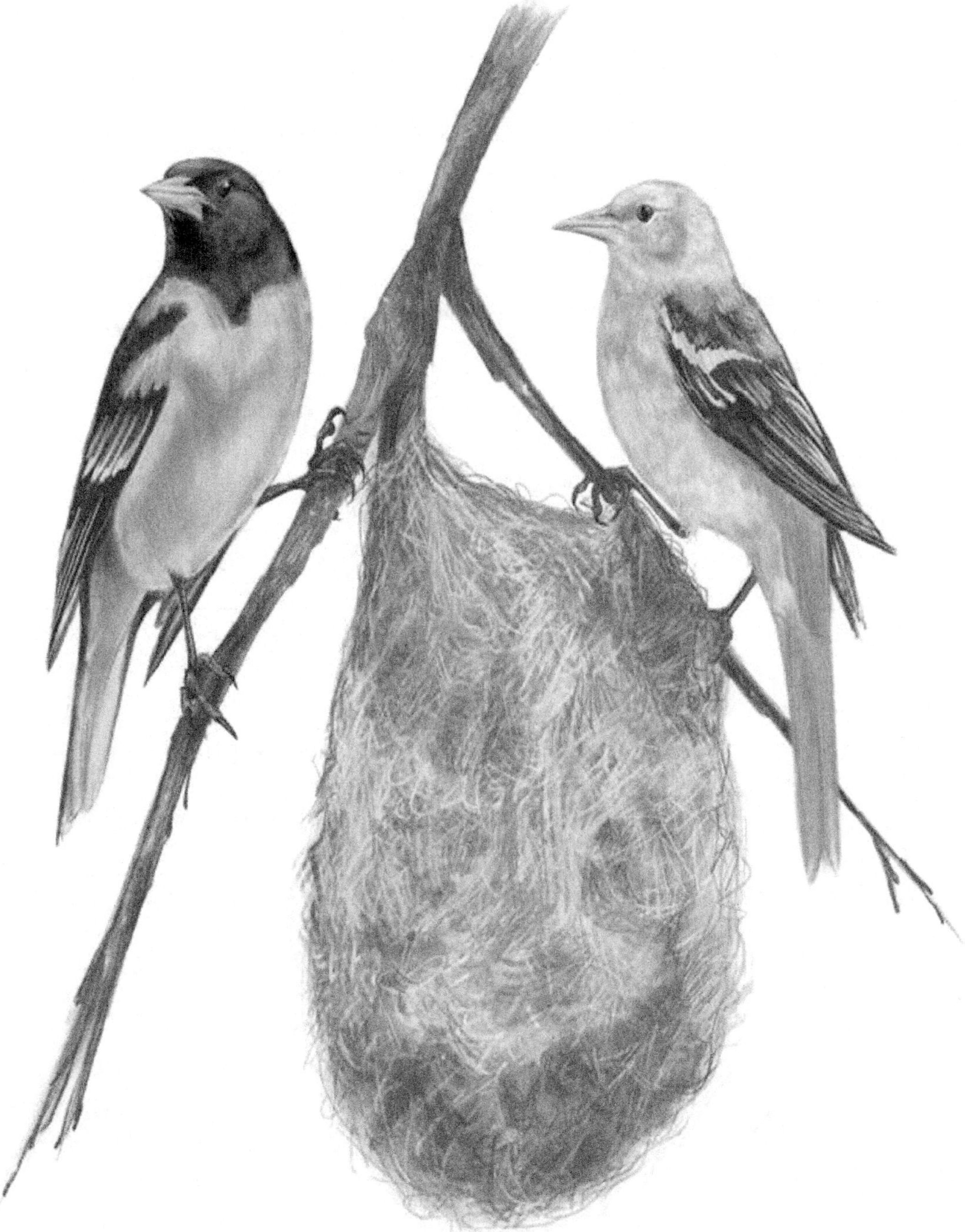

Male and female

GENERAL INFORMATION

- **Male:** A medium-sized orange bird with all-black head, wings, back, and tail.
- **Female:** A medium-sized orange-washed bird with darker back and wings.
- **Range:** Found from the Plains states eastward.
- **Migration:** Winters in Florida, migrates through southern part of range, breeds in northern part of range.
- **Preferred Food:** Berries, fruit, jelly, mealworms, nectar, suet.
- **Preferred Feeders:** Fruit/jelly feeder, nectar, suet feeder, wire mesh (mealworms).
- **Nesting:**
  - **Natural:** A pouch made from plant fibers and hair hanging from a tree branch.
  - **Man-made:** Will not nest in man-made structures.
- **Eggs:** Light beige with brown swirls, approximately 1" long.

TIPS FOR ATTRACTING

- The Baltimore Oriole is a common backyard visitor, and by providing fruit and jelly, you will hopefully encourage it to visit your feeders and birdbaths.
- Supply only enough fruit and jelly for one day's consumption to avoid problems with wasps and ants.
- Maintain feeding them until they leave to help them prepare for migration.

IN YOUR YARD

If you have Baltimore Orioles in your yard, enjoy them while you can. They will begin their southward migration beginning in July, earlier than most other songbirds. When you have learned their song, be sure to check high in trees to spot them. If there is orange on the cheek with an orange eye stripe, you most likely have the common western oriole, the Bullock's Oriole (*Icterus bullockii*), found in the Plains states westward.

Bewick's Wren
Thryomanes bewickii

Male and female Bewick's Wrens are identical in appearance.

GENERAL INFORMATION

- **Male:** A small bird with short, angled, and barred tail; dull-brown back; and prominent creamy eye stripe.
- **Female:** The female Bewick's Wren is not visibly different from the male.
- **Range:** Found in southern-central US and West Coast states.
- **Migration:** Found year-round in its range.
- **Preferred Food:** Fruit, insects, mealworms, peanut hearts, suet.
- **Preferred Feeders:** Fruit/jelly feeder, hopper feeder, suet feeder, tray feeder, wire mesh (fruit, mealworms).
- **Nesting:**
  - **Natural:** Nests in natural cavities or man-made objects, including crevices in walls, tin cans, and mailboxes.

- **Man-made:** 4" D × 4" W × 8" H nest box, 1 ¼"-diameter hole 2" down from the top, placed 5"–10" off the ground.
* **Eggs:** Creamy with spotting more toward the large end, approximately ⅝" long.

TIPS FOR ATTRACTING

* **If Bewick's Wrens are present in your area in the winter season, you may want to supply seed that has fruit and berries to provide balanced nutrition.**
* **Plant shrubs and thickets like elderberry, sumac, and typical chaparral species so wrens can enjoy the berries and insects found in those plants.**
* **Wrens like water sources a lot, so offering several choices like ground and pedestal birdbaths with drippers or misters may draw them to your yard.**

IN YOUR YARD

Bewick's Wrens will often associate with chickadees and nuthatches. If these species are present in your yard, you may want to consider plantings, food, and birdhouses to attract wrens to visit and nest there. They will also appreciate a brush pile if you have the space for one in your yard. Bewick's Wrens are small and wary birds and may need a little time to become comfortable in a new setting. Once familiar with your yard, they will become a common sight.

Black-capped Chickadee
Poecile atricapillus

Male and female Black-capped Chickadees are identical in appearance.

GENERAL INFORMATION

- **Male:** A small vocal bird with black cap and chin, white face, gray back, and creamy breast.
- **Female:** The female Black-capped Chickadee is not visibly different from the male.
- **Range:** Found in the northern half of the US.
- **Migration:** Found year-round in its range.
- **Preferred Food:** Mealworms, peanuts, peanut hearts, safflower seed, suet, sunflower seed.
- **Preferred Feeders:** Hopper feeder, suet feeder, tray feeder, tube feeder, wire mesh (mealworms, peanuts).
- **Nesting:**
  - **Natural:** A cavity usually in a birch or pine tree, less than 10' from the ground.
  - **Man-made:** 4" D × 4" W × 8" H nest box, 1 1/8"-diameter hole 2" down from the top, wood shavings on the floor, placed 4'–15' off the ground.

- **Eggs:** Creamy white with spotting more toward the large end, approximately ⅝" long.

TIPS FOR ATTRACTING

- Place chickadee houses for nesting in a partly sunny, wooded area. If placed closer to a cleared area, the nest box may attract wrens instead.
- Black-capped Chickadees are inquisitive, and providing a variety of its favorite seeds will make it one of the first visitors to your yard.
- Many other small birds associate with chickadees, and they will help to draw other birds to your feeders.

IN YOUR YARD

The very similar-looking Carolina Chickadee (*Poecile carolinensis*) is the southeastern counterpart to the Black-capped Chickadee. Chickadees are generally very comfortable being near people. Given time and patience, they can be taught to take seed from your hand. They can frequently be seen taking seeds and flying off to a tree or shrub to cache the seed for later consumption.

Black-chinned Hummingbird
Archilochus alexandri

Male and female

GENERAL INFORMATION

- **Male:** A tiny bird with greenish back, dusky belly, violet throat, and black chin.
- **Female:** A tiny bird with greenish back and whitish belly.
- **Range:** Found in most states west of the Plains states.
- **Migration:** Summer breeding in range, some limited migration through California and the Northwest.
- **Preferred Food:** Nectar, naturally occurring nectar flowers.
- **Preferred Feeders:** Nectar.
- **Nesting:**
  - **Natural:** A tiny nest made from plant down, usually 5'–10' off the ground and near water.
  - **Man-made:** Will not nest in man-made structures.

- **Eggs:** Unmarked white eggs, approximately ⅜" long.

TIPS FOR ATTRACTING

- Add red-, orange-, or pink-flowered plants to gardens that are known to attract Black-chinned Hummingbirds, such as bee balm, phlox, and hollyhock.
- Be sure to keep the feeders full if you have numerous hummingbirds since they have a very high metabolism and need to feed about every ten minutes to survive.
- Hummingbirds like to visit birdbaths with misters to bathe in and then preen afterward.

IN YOUR YARD

A hummingbird's courtship display flight is enjoyable to watch; the male will swoop and arc repeatedly a short distance from the female. Contrary to a common misconception, keeping hummingbird feeders up late in the season will not delay a bird's migration. It is better to keep feeders out so they can fuel up for their long flights, after which you can remove feeders for the season.

Blue Jay
Cyanocitta cristata

Male and female Blue Jays are identical in appearance.

GENERAL INFORMATION

- **Male:** A larger-crested songbird with blue upper body and white underbelly, with black and white markings on its head and tail.
- **Female:** The female Blue Jay is not visibly different from the male.
- **Range:** Found in the US from the Plains states eastward.
- **Migration:** Found year-round in its range.
- **Preferred Food:** Cracked corn, peanuts, suet, sunflower seed.
- **Preferred Feeders:** Hopper feeder, suet feeder, tray feeder, tube feeder.
- **Nesting:**
  - **Natural:** Found in trees 10'–20' high, made of twigs and grass.
  - **Man-made:** Will not nest in man-made structures.
- **Eggs:** Light blue with brownish spots, approximately 1" long.

TIPS FOR ATTRACTING

- **Blue Jays like to survey the area first before heading to the feeders, so placing feeders near trees will provide them with a perch to check things out.**
- **Having tray feeders is the quickest way to get this species to come to your backyard.**
- **Place suet or suet cakes where Blue Jays can perch to eat.**
- **Blue Jays are one of the birds that can eat unshelled peanuts, but this could attract more squirrels and be a little messier.**

IN YOUR YARD

Some people do not like Blue Jays at their feeders because of their sometimes "aggressive" behavior. True, they are a species that likes to come to feeders and get their share of seed and are not afraid to temporarily displace a bird or two. If this becomes a problem, you can relocate the tray or hopper feeder away from other feeders. However, Blue Jays are one of the few birds at your feeder that will sound the alarm to alert all your avian visitors that a cat, hawk, or other possible predator is nearby.

Brown-headed Cowbird
Molothrus ater

Male and female

GENERAL INFORMATION

- **Male:** A medium-sized bird with black body and dark brown head.
- **Female:** A medium-sized, uniformly dull-gray-brown bird with heavy, thick bill.
- **Range:** Found throughout the US.
- **Migration:** Year-round in the southern half of the US, summer breeding in the northern half.
- **Preferred Food:** Cracked corn, millet, peanut hearts, sunflower seed.
- **Preferred Feeders:** Ground forager, hopper feeder, tray feeder.
- **Nesting:**
  - **Natural:** None; the Brown-headed Cowbird lays its eggs in the nests of other birds to have the host species incubate and raise its young.
  - **Man-made:** Will not nest in man-made structures.

- **Eggs:** Pale creamy green with heavy splotching, approximately ⅞" long.

TIPS FOR ATTRACTING

- **Scattering preferred foods directly on the ground is the best placement of food for Brown-headed Cowbirds.**
- **If you live in a cowbird's summer range, you may notice fewer feeding visits due to a natural and seasonal shift in diet from seed to insects.**

IN YOUR YARD

Depending on your location, you may have a few cowbirds or larger flocks. If you would like to discourage visits by cowbirds, you will need to alter your food options. These birds are mostly ground foragers, so limiting what seed you place on the ground will help keep them away, along with removing tray feeders. Many people do not like cowbirds because of their nesting strategy. Cowbird nestlings usually grow faster and larger than their host species' nestlings. As a result, the offspring of the host may not survive, and their populations are reduced.

Brown Thrasher
Toxostoma rufum

Male and female Brown Thrashers are identical in appearance.

GENERAL INFORMATION

- **Male:** A larger bird with rusty-brown crown, back, wings, and tail; has a heavily dark-spotted creamy breast.
- **Female:** The female Brown Thrasher is not visibly different from the male.
- **Range:** Found in Plains states and eastward.
- **Migration:** Year-round in its southern range, summer breeding in its northern range.
- **Preferred Food:** Fruits, dehydrated fruits, mealworms, suet, sunflower seed.
- **Preferred Feeders:** Fruit/jelly feeder, hopper feeder, suet feeder, tray feeder, wire mesh (fruit, mealworms).
- **Nesting:**
  - **Natural:** Usually found less than 10' off the ground in shrubs, made from layered twigs and leaves.
  - **Man-made:** Will not nest in man-made structures.
- **Eggs:** Creamy beige with brown splotching, approximately 1" long.

TIPS FOR ATTRACTING

- **One way to attract these birds to your backyard habitat is by having dense thickets and hedges, which the Brown Thrasher will forage and hide in.**
- **Thrashers will eat fruit from bushes in the fall and winter, so planting fruit-bearing species may attract them to your yard if the habitat is right.**
- **Place the appropriate feeder closer to the ground to increase the likelihood of thrashers visiting to eat.**

IN YOUR YARD

Brown Thrashers will mimic other birds' songs and some noises from the human world. Often these phrases are repeated two or three times each. Two other birds that do this are the catbird and the mockingbird. You may hear the Brown Thrasher more than you see it because it is secretive in its environment, eating lower to the ground, quickly perching in the open, and then retreating again.

Bushtit
Psaltriparus minimus

Male and female

GENERAL INFORMATION

- **Male:** A small, overall grayish bird with a dark eye, the breast being slightly lighter.
- **Female:** A small, overall grayish-brown bird with a yellow eye, the breast being slightly lighter.
- **Range:** Found in western US.
- **Migration:** Found year-round in its range.
- **Preferred Food:** Mealworms, peanuts, peanut hearts, suet, sunflower seed.
- **Preferred Feeders:** Hopper feeder, suet feeder, tray feeder, tube feeder, wire mesh (mealworms, peanuts).
- **Nesting:**
  - **Natural:** A pouch made from roots, moss, and leaves suspended from a branch usually 5'–25' off the ground.

- ○ **Man-made:** Will not nest in man-made structures.
- **Eggs:** Unmarked white eggs, approximately ½" long.

TIPS FOR ATTRACTING

- Planting native regional shrubs will make your yard similar to the Bushtit's natural environment, and they will forage with small flocks of other species.
- Offer a variety of foods that the Bushtit will eat or that is suitable for other species that it associates with, such as kinglets and chickadees.

IN YOUR YARD

The Bushtit is a nondescript little bird and may be overlooked because of its size and coloring. When feeding flocks pass through your area, be sure to check for a Bushtit to be mingling with them. Many people have experienced a mass of Bushtits descending onto the feeders. Enjoy watching them do acrobatic maneuvers similar to chickadees while getting food from your feeders.

Carolina Wren
Thryothorus ludovicianus

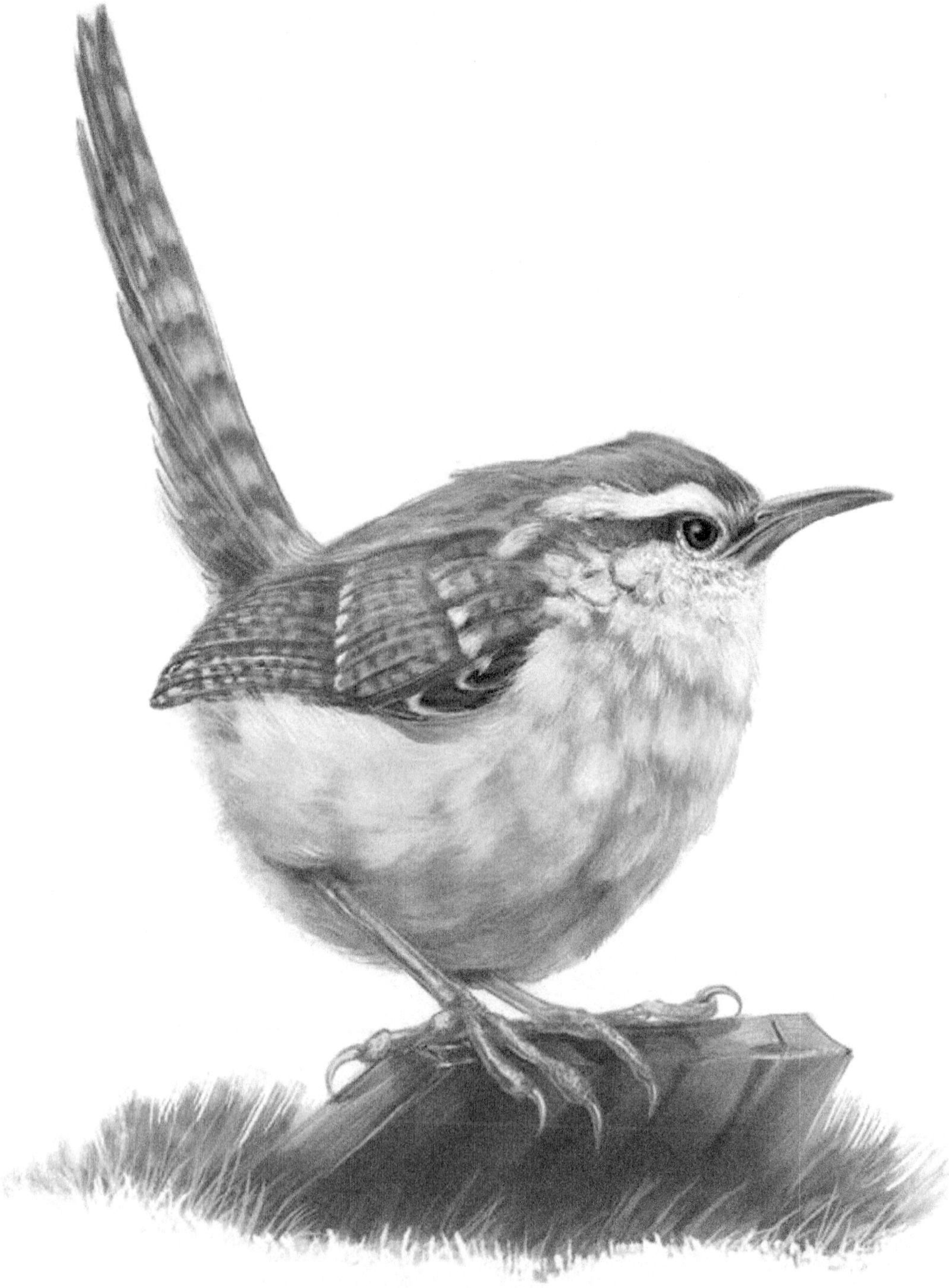

Male and female Carolina Wrens are identical in appearance.

GENERAL INFORMATION

- **Male:** A small bird with brown cap, back, wings, and tail; white eye stripe; and beige belly.
- **Female:** The female Carolina Wren is not visibly different from the male.
- **Range:** Found in eastern US south of New England states.
- **Migration:** Found year-round in its range with little migration.
- **Preferred Food:** Hulled sunflower seed, mealworms, peanuts, suet.
- **Preferred Feeders:** Hopper feeder, suet feeder, tray feeder, tube feeder, wire mesh (mealworms, peanuts).
- **Nesting:**
    - **Natural:** Made in natural cavities or larger man-made objects with cavities, such as pails and baskets.
    - **Man-made:** 4" D × 5" W × 7" H nesting box with a tilted roof, front panel shorter at the top by 1 ½", placed 5'–10' off the ground.
- **Eggs:** Cream-colored with brown mostly at the larger end, approximately ¾" long.

TIPS FOR ATTRACTING

- **This wren is commonly found around human habitation and will feed, bathe, and nest in yards.**
- **The Carolina Wren will eat fruits and berries in winter, so having fruiting vegetation would be a great lure to bring this species to your backyard.**
- **As with all wrens, a brush pile or dense shrubs will seem like home to the Carolina Wren.**

IN YOUR YARD

The Carolina Wren's song can sometimes be confused for a Northern Cardinal. Even if you recognize its song, it may take some time to actually see this small bird. It can perch high and low while singing, which makes it even harder to spot. Attracting Carolina Wrens to your yard for nesting might take some time, but you can definitely entice them with many found-item nest sites. They are known to shelter in nesting boxes in the winter if you are in a cold locale.

Chipping Sparrow
Spizella passerina

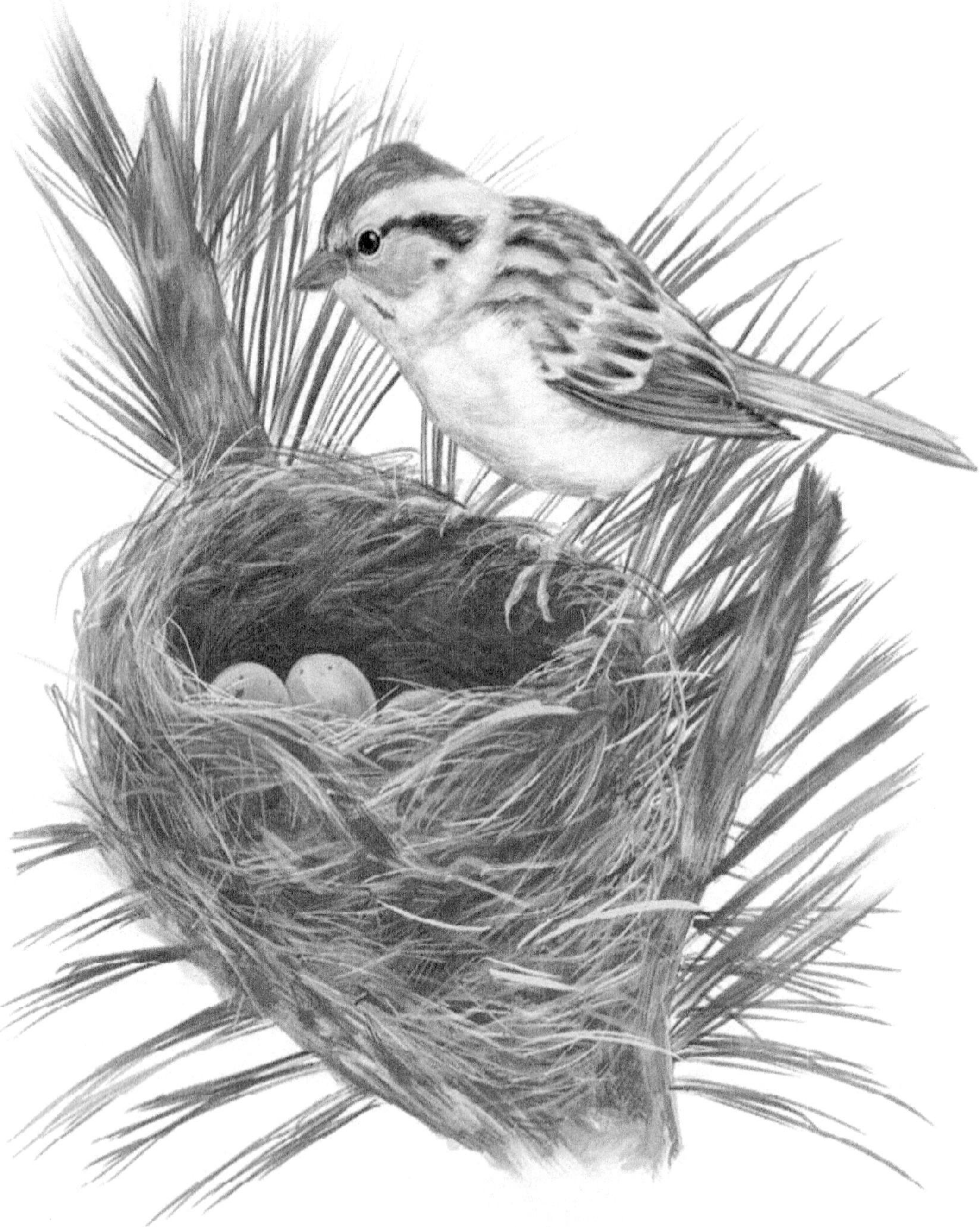

Male and female Chipping Sparrows are identical in appearance.

GENERAL INFORMATION

- **Male:** A small light-gray-breasted bird with rufous cap and black eye stripe. Its back is brown with black striping.
- **Female:** The female Chipping Sparrow is not visibly different from the male.
- **Range:** Found throughout the US.
- **Migration:** Winters in Florida and in extreme Southwest, breeds elsewhere in its range.
- **Preferred Food:** Cracked corn, hulled sunflower seed, millet, Nyjer seed.
- **Preferred Feeders:** Ground forager, hopper feeder, tray feeder.
- **Nesting:**
  - **Natural:** Usually in a conifer tree, 1'–10' above the ground, cuplike, and made of grass and animal hair.
  - **Man-made:** Will not nest in man-made structures.
- **Eggs:** Light blue with scattered brown spotting, approximately ¾" long.

TIPS FOR ATTRACTING

- **Chipping Sparrows are very common and will visit your yard if you provide ground food, especially millet and cracked corn.**
- **Having some conifers or small shrubs in your yard will increase your chance of having these birds nest in your yard.**
- **Chipping Sparrows prefer being closer to the ground, so having a birdbath on the ground will draw them in more than a pedestal style.**

IN YOUR YARD

For many people, the sparrow is a sign of spring. Many birds associated with spring can come back north quite early, but the Chipping Sparrow will hold out until the weather really does start warming up. Individuals are easily visible singing from an obvious perch, usually at the end of a tree branch. They are a beneficial species to have in your yard since insects make up a majority of their diet during nesting season.

Common Grackle
Quiscalus quiscula

Male and female

GENERAL INFORMATION

- **Male:** A larger, long-tailed black bird with an iridescent-purple head.
- **Female:** A larger, long-tailed dull-black bird.
- **Range:** Found east of the Rockies.
- **Migration:** Found year-round in most of the eastern US, summer breeding in northern and western part of range.
- **Preferred Food:** Cracked corn, fruit, peanuts, peanut hearts, sunflower seed.
- **Preferred Feeders:** Ground forager, hopper feeder, tray feeder.
- **Nesting:**
    - **Natural:** Made from twigs and stalks, found in variable locations, including conifers and shrubs in parks.
    - **Man-made:** Will not nest in man-made structures.

- **Eggs:** Light blue with brown spotting and swirling, approximately 1 ⅛" long.

TIPS FOR ATTRACTING

- **Grackles are one of those birds that will show up to your feeders, whether invited or not. They are general seed eaters and will take food from a variety of feeders and are not too picky about what type of food they eat.**

IN YOUR YARD

For some backyard bird enthusiasts, Common Grackles can quickly wear out their welcome in spring by dominating feeders by their numbers and actions. If you would like to discourage them from becoming the dominant species at your feeders, either alter the food you offer or the type of feeder you use. Since they are a larger bird, they need a larger feeder to perch at, so removing tray feeders for a while will help to diminish their control. They will tolerate using tube feeders even though it may not be their first choice. Since grackles are voracious eaters, using cages around tube feeders also works wonders and reduces the quantity of seed you need to purchase.

Dark-eyed Junco
Junco hyemalis

Male and female

GENERAL INFORMATION

- **Male:** A small sparrow-sized bird with charcoal-gray upper body and white lower body and white outer tail feathers.
- **Female:** The female Dark-eyed Junco has a similar pattern but with charcoal-brown upper body and white belly.
- **Range:** Found throughout the US.
- **Migration:** Found year-round in the Rockies and New England, winter resident elsewhere.
- **Preferred Food:** Cracked corn, millet, Nyjer seed, peanut hearts, safflower seed, sunflower seed.
- **Preferred Feeders:** Ground forager, hopper feeder, tray feeder.
- **Nesting:**

- **Natural:** A cuplike nest on the ground, hidden by stumps, roots, or overhanging vegetation.
  - **Man-made:** Will not nest in man-made structures.
- **Eggs:** Pale blue with brown splotching and a "ring" at the large end, approximately ¾" long.

TIPS FOR ATTRACTING

- **Juncos will predominantly feed from the ground, so scattering seed on the ground will draw them to your yard.**
- **While they may perch in trees, juncos like to have a little cover between trips to the feeder for food. Adding a brush pile will make your yard more attractive to them.**
- **Juncos are a common winter bird, so providing a heated birdbath will make your backyard more inviting as a winter source of water.**

IN YOUR YARD

For many backyard birders, this species is the first sign that autumn is coming. The Dark-eyed Junco will usually stay throughout winter, just like the American Tree Sparrow. The white outer tail feathers that show when the bird is in flight make it easy to recognize, even from a distance. There are several subspecies across the country with color variations. A field guide will sort out those subspecies and their respective field marks.

Downy Woodpecker
Dryobates pubescens

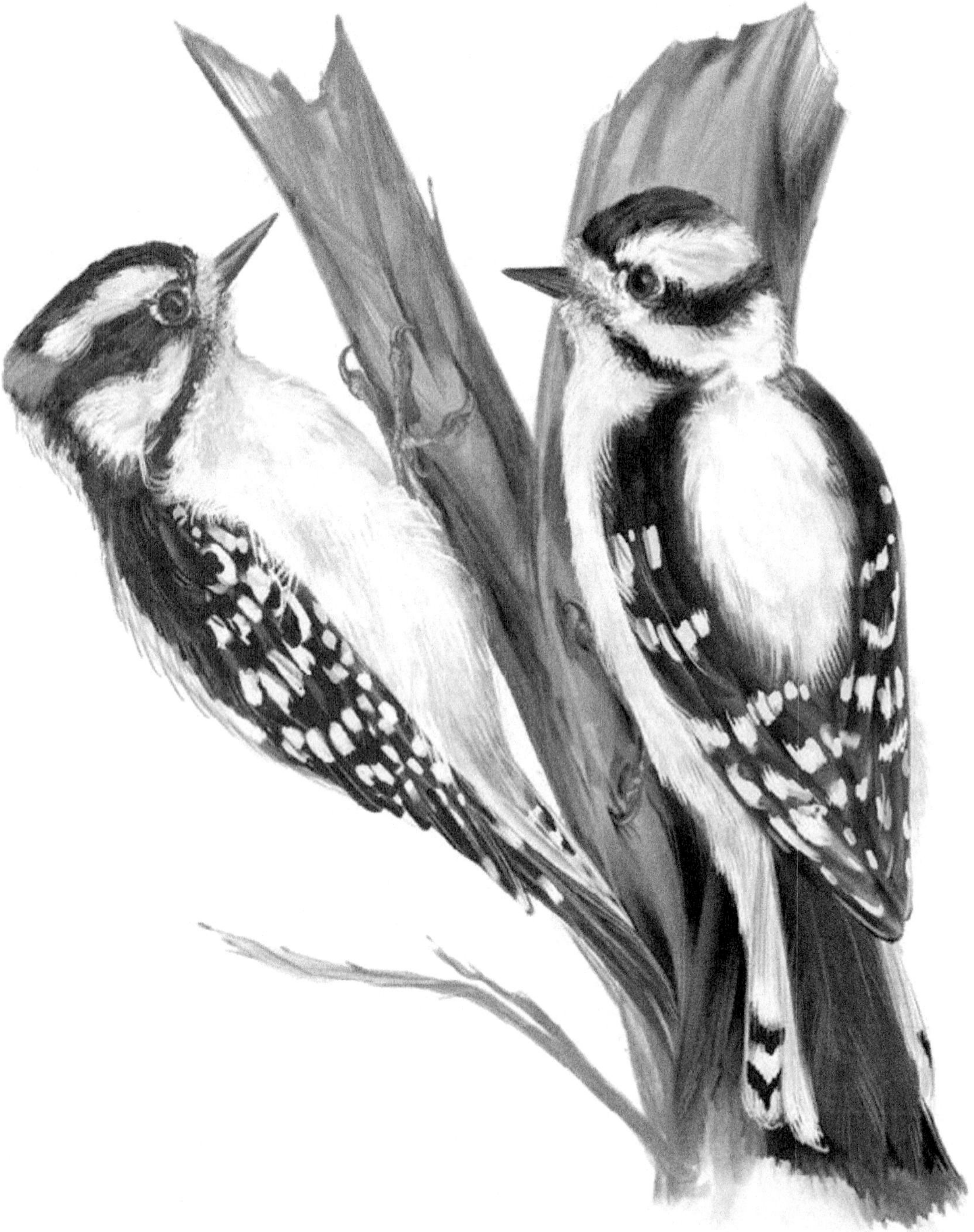

Male and female

GENERAL INFORMATION

- **Male:** A tree-climbing black-and-white bird with a red spot on the back of the head and black spots on the white outer tail feathers.
- **Female:** The female Downy Woodpecker is nearly identical to the male but does not have the red spot on the back of the head.
- **Range:** Found in all of the US except the southern edge of southwestern states.
- **Migration:** Found year-round in its range.
- **Preferred Food:** Mealworms, peanuts, safflower seed, suet, sunflower seed.
- **Preferred Feeders:** Hopper feeder, suet feeder, tray feeder, tube feeder, wire mesh (mealworms, peanuts).
- **Nesting:**
  - **Natural:** A cavity nest in a tree, 5'–40' off the ground.
  - **Man-made:** 4" D × 4" W × 12" H nest box, 1 ½"-diameter hole 2" down from the top, placed 5'–20' off the ground with wood chips placed on the floor.
- **Eggs:** Unmarked white eggs, approximately ⅞" long.

TIPS FOR ATTRACTING

- **The Downy Woodpecker is sure to be one of your yard visitors, provided you have suet or sunflower seed at your feeders.**
- **To encourage productive visits to your yard, have feeders with no perches, as these will be almost exclusively used by woodpeckers and chickadees.**
- **Downy Woodpeckers can be a little timid or bothered by other birds, so placing feeders just for woodpeckers (especially suet) away from the main feeders may make them feel more at ease.**

IN YOUR YARD

Downy Woodpeckers will usually come to a feeder, grab some food, and eat it on a nearby branch and then return for more. You may have heard the Downy Woodpecker drumming (tapping) on trees. Each woodpecker has a different drumming rhythm, and because this species is so common, you will probably learn its pattern.

Eastern Bluebird
Sialia sialis

Male and female

GENERAL INFORMATION

- **Male:** A medium-sized bird with a sky-blue back and head, with rusty breast.
- **Female:** The female is very similar to the male except its colors are much more muted.
- **Range:** Found east of the Plains states.
- **Migration:** Found year-round in the southern half of its range, summer breeding in the northern half.
- **Preferred Food:** Fruit, mealworms, peanut hearts, suet.
- **Preferred Feeders:** Ground forager, fruit/jelly feeder, suet feeder, tray feeder, wire mesh (fruit, mealworms).
- **Nesting:**
  - **Natural:** A cavity nest in a tree, stump, or old woodpecker nest sites.
  - **Man-made:** 5" D × 5" W × 10" H nest box, 1 ½"-diameter hole 2" down from the top, placed 4'–6' off the ground.

- **Eggs:** Unmarked blue, approximately ⅞" long.

TIPS FOR ATTRACTING

- **Bluebirds are usually found in more open-area habitats. If you are in an area where bluebirds are found, providing birdhouses will be key in attracting them to your location.**
- **Place birdhouses on posts in open areas 4'–6' above the ground, facing the opening away from the sun and wind.**
- **You will need to provide the preferred food sources to attract them. Eastern Bluebirds are not seed eaters, so you may need to purchase the listed foods and feeders if you have been using only typical bird feeders.**

IN YOUR YARD

Bluebirds are cavity nesters, unlike the other members of the thrush family. The abundance of House Sparrows and starlings has had a negative impact on bluebirds, since they also nest in cavities. The more assertive behavior of these other two species will drive bluebirds away from potential nesting sites. Making sure birdhouses have the appropriate entrance size will help deter House Sparrows and starlings. Through the efforts of the North American Bluebird Society and its members, the bluebird population has been rising again.

Eastern Phoebe
Sayornis phoebe

Male and female Eastern Phoebes are identical in appearance.

GENERAL INFORMATION

- **Male:** A medium-sized bird with white belly and throat and dull gray-brown head, back, and tail. Phoebes bob their tails up and down while perched.
- **Female:** The female Eastern Phoebe is not visibly different from the male.
- **Range:** Found in the Plains states and eastward.
- **Migration:** Found year-round in the southern states, summer resident in the northern range, winter resident along the Gulf Coast.
- **Preferred Food:** Mostly flying insects, some fruit during migration.
- **Preferred Feeders:** Will not come to feeders.
- **Nesting:**
  - **Natural:** Made of mud, moss, and other vegetation on eaves of buildings, barns, or bridges.
  - **Man-made:** 7" D × 7" W × 7" H shelf style, with sloped roof and 2 sides open, placed 5'–15' off the ground.
- **Eggs:** Unmarked creamy, approximately ¾" long.

TIPS FOR ATTRACTING

- **While not a feeder bird, Eastern Phoebes are common nesters in backyard habitats and may come to birdbaths.**
- **Providing shelf platforms for nesting will encourage this insect eater to take up residence in your yard.**
- **The phoebe is one of the earlier spring migrants, and you should have potential nesting shelves up early enough in the nesting season.**

IN YOUR YARD

The Eastern Phoebe is one of the common flycatchers you will see and hear. Flycatchers are a family of birds that find preferred perches to hunt from, repeatedly going after insects and returning to the same perch. Along with being an early spring arrival, they are one of the last flycatchers to migrate southward. Phoebes are also one of the few flycatchers to winter in the southern US.

Eurasian Collared-Dove
Streptopelia decaocto

Male and female Eurasian Collared-Doves are identical in appearance.

GENERAL INFORMATION

- **Male:** A larger, overall pale gray bird with darker wing tips and a black crescent on the back of the neck.
- **Female:** The female Eurasian Collared-Dove is not visibly different from the male.
- **Range:** Found in all of the western, central, and southern states.
- **Migration:** Found year-round in its range.
- **Preferred Food:** Cracked corn, millet, peanut hearts, sunflower seed.
- **Preferred Feeders:** Ground forager, hopper feeder, tray feeder.
- **Nesting:**
  - **Natural:** Made of sticks in trees or shrubs or sometimes on buildings.
  - **Man-made:** Will not nest in man-made structures.
- **Eggs:** White unmarked, approximately 1 ⅛" long.

TIPS FOR ATTRACTING

- If you live within the range of the Eurasian Collared-Dove, it is most likely to visit your yard as long as the food is placed on the ground or in low tray feeders.
- Doves are typically ground foragers and will be looking for a variety of spilled seed from the other birds visiting your feeders.
- These doves prefer birdbaths that are on the ground and shallower than normal.

IN YOUR YARD

The Eurasian Collared-Dove is a recent arrival to North America. It was introduced from Cuba, arrived in Florida in the late 1980s, and has already established itself all the way to the West Coast. As with some introduced species, like the European Starling and the House Sparrow, this dove can sometimes become so abundant as to become a pest.

European Starling
Sturnus vulgaris

Male and female European Starlings are identical in appearance.

GENERAL INFORMATION

- **Male:** A medium-sized black bird with iridescent body, white spotting on back, and yellow bill. A dark bill and more spotting are present in winter.
- **Female:** The female European Starling is not visibly different from the male.
- **Range:** Found throughout the US.
- **Migration:** Found year-round in its range.
- **Preferred Food:** Cracked corn, millet, suet, sunflower seed.
- **Preferred Feeders:** Ground forager, any feeder it can perch on.
- **Nesting:**
  - **Natural:** A cavity nest found in trees or man-made structures.
  - **Man-made:** Providing nest boxes is discouraged.
- **Eggs:** Light blue unmarked, approximately 1 1/8" long.

TIPS FOR ATTRACTING

- **The European Starling is an introduced bird from Europe and has become a pest species in North America.**
- **Starlings will visit your feeders if you live in urban and suburban settings and offer their preferred food.**
- **To discourage them from coming to your feeders, shorten perches and provide less-preferred foods in specific feeders, such as safflower seed and Nyjer seed.**
- **Another way to discourage European Starlings from coming to your feeders is to use feeders with cages to exclude access to starlings but allow smaller birds to get to the food.**

IN YOUR YARD

European Starlings are one of the main causes for the decline of some native species, along with the House Sparrow. They will displace native cavity-nesting species from natural nest sites, and if the opening of a birdhouse is more than 1 ½", the starling will be able to nest in the box. Starlings are also gregarious and will come in small or large flocks to eat at feeders. They are voracious, and if you don't have some way of discouraging them from eating at your feeders, they will quickly be emptied.

Fox Sparrow
Passerella iliaca

Male and female Fox Sparrows are identical in appearance.

GENERAL INFORMATION

- **Male:** A rusty-brown sparrow with heavy spotting on the breast, mixed with gray striping on the head and back.
- **Female:** The female Fox Sparrow is not visibly different from the male.
- **Range:** Found in all of the US except the Southwest.
- **Migration:** Winters along the West Coast and the lower southeastern states, two subspecies breed in California and the Northwest, otherwise migrates through the northern half of the US east of the Plains states.
- **Preferred Food:** Corn, millet, sunflower seed.
- **Preferred Feeders:** Ground forager, hopper feeder, tray feeder.
- **Nesting:**
  - **Natural:** A nest with outer layer assembled from small twigs and lined with softer natural grasses and moss.
  - **Man-made:** Will not nest in man-made structures.

- **Eggs:** Blue-green with heavy splotching, approximately 1" long.

TIPS FOR ATTRACTING

- Since the Fox Sparrow is a ground forager, make sure you have seed available on the ground for winter and migration feeding.
- Like most sparrows, the Fox Sparrow will feel more comfortable in yards with brush or shrubs present for cover.
- For plantings, hawthorn trees and blackberry and raspberry bushes are particular favorites of the Fox Sparrow.

IN YOUR YARD

This bird looks very similar to the Song Sparrow to those who are just starting to watch birds in their backyards. The more reddish tones overall and the larger size are the main identifying features of the Fox Sparrow. This species may be present in your area seasonally, but it may take more searching to see because of its secretive nature compared to other sparrows that will visit your backyard. For those in the Northwest, you will be fortunate to see and hear the Fox Sparrows year-round, since they also breed in your region.

Gray Catbird
Dumetella carolinensis

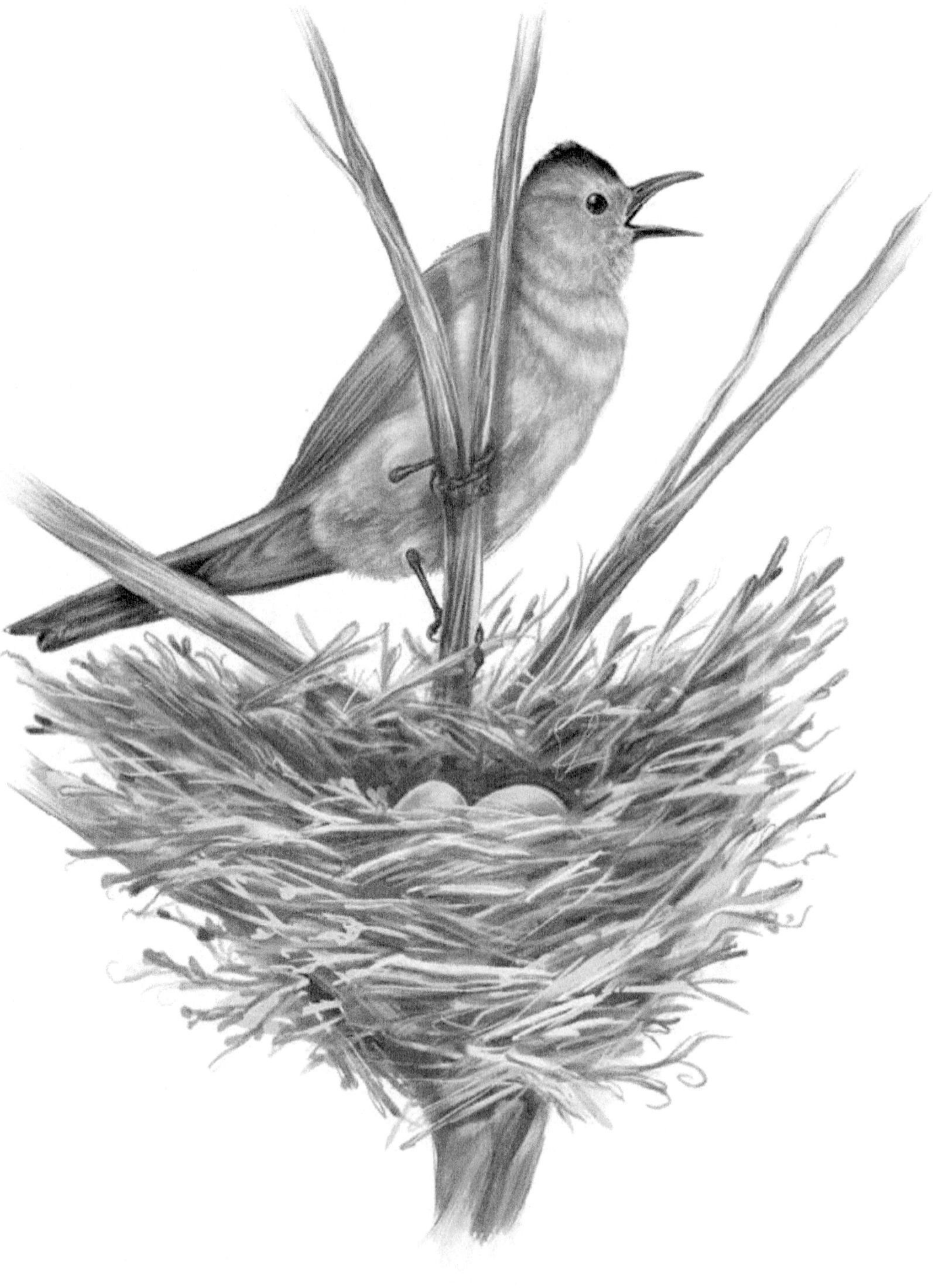

Male and female Gray Catbirds are identical in appearance.

GENERAL INFORMATION

- **Male:** A dark gray bird with black cap and rusty undertail.
- **Female:** The female Gray Catbird is not visibly different from the male.
- **Range:** Found throughout US except for Southwest and southern Plains states.
- **Migration:** Winters in Gulf states, year-round interior Gulf states and mid-Atlantic coast, migrates through Texas, breeds elsewhere in its range.
- **Preferred Food:** Fruit, suet.
- **Preferred Feeders:** Fruit/jelly feeder, suet feeder.
- **Nesting:**
  - **Natural:** A nest made with lots of twigs and lined with grasses and needles, placed in shrubby vegetation.
  - **Man-made:** Will not nest in man-made structures.
- **Eggs:** Light blue unmarked, approximately 1" long.

TIPS FOR ATTRACTING

- Make sure to have a fruit/jelly feeder out for the Gray Catbird if you would like this species to visit your yard frequently. Chopped-up pieces of fruit are an added attraction.
- Planting denser berry-producing shrubs and hedges will definitely bring the Gray Catbird in for a closer look, and it will normally spend most of its time among this type of foliage.
- A water feature such as a birdbath or pond with dripping water will also make your backyard sanctuary more appealing to the catbird.

IN YOUR YARD

Most likely you will hear the Gray Catbirds before you see them. They are very vocal, making all kinds of squeaky noises and actually sounding like a cat sometimes, hence the common name. Catbirds are related to the Northern Mockingbird and the Brown Thrasher, and all three mimic other birds to some degree. Catbirds like to hide in denser vegetation, but they will allow you to get closer to observe them without flying away. Investing in fruiting shrubs and trees for catbirds will benefit you by attracting other fruit-loving birds discussed in this book.

Hairy Woodpecker
Dryobates villosus

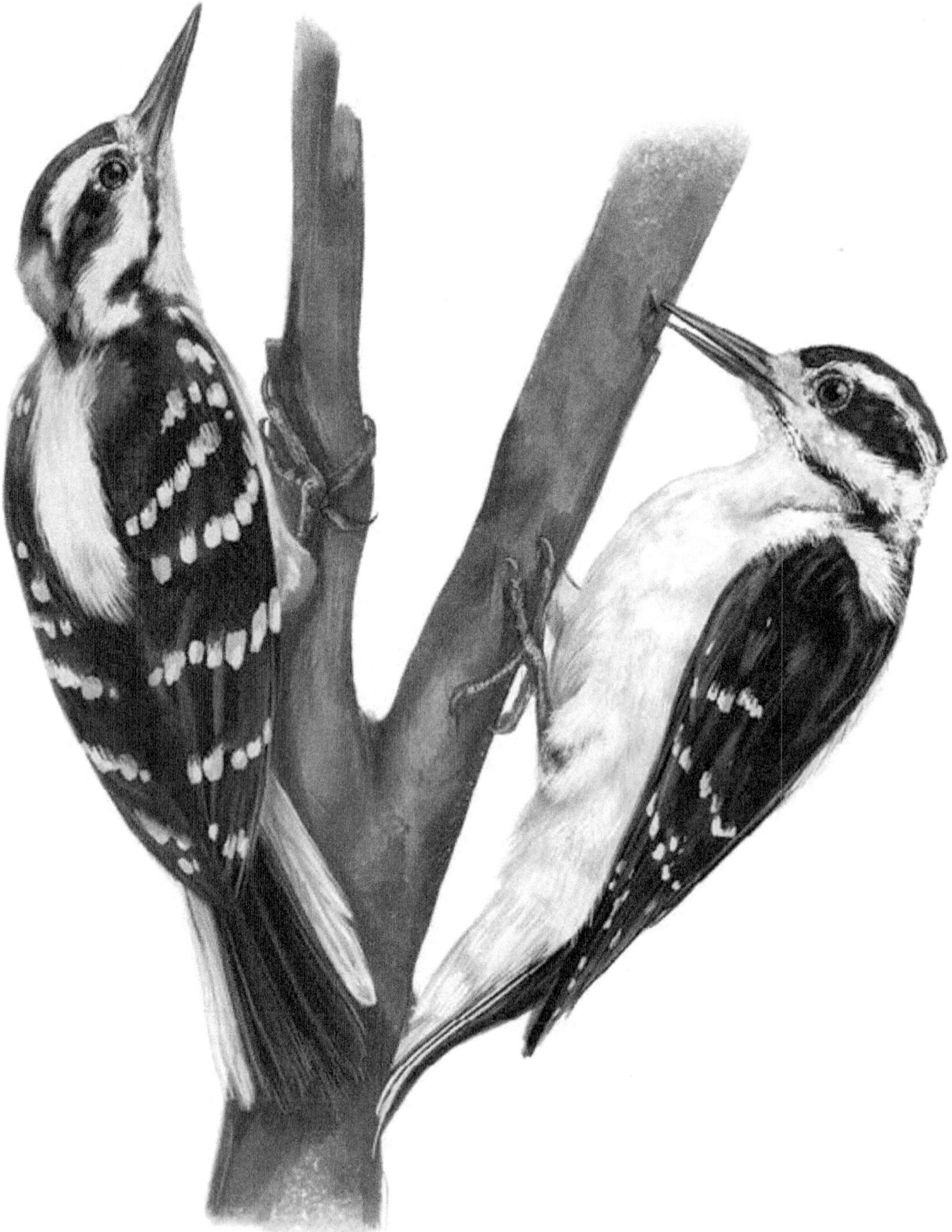

Male and female

GENERAL INFORMATION

- **Male:** A tree-climbing black-and-white bird with a red spot on the back of the head and all white on the outer tail feathers.
- **Female:** The female Hairy Woodpecker is nearly identical to the male but does not have the red spot on the back of the head.
- **Range:** Found in all of the US except some locations in Texas and the West Coast states.
- **Migration:** Found year-round in its range.
- **Preferred Food:** Peanuts, suet, sunflower seed.
- **Preferred Feeders:** Suet feeder, tube feeder, wire mesh (peanuts).
- **Nesting:**
  - **Natural:** A cavity nest found in dead trees or branches, which it will excavate.
  - **Man-made:** 6" D × 6" W × 14" H nest box, 1 ½"-diameter hole, placed 8'–20' off the ground on a tree with wood chips placed in the box.
- **Eggs:** White unmarked, approximately 1" long.

TIPS FOR ATTRACTING

- **The three preferred foods listed will almost guarantee the Hairy Woodpecker's presence in your yard.**
- **Providing food in winter will help the Hairy Woodpecker in years when the natural food supply is insufficient and they are searching for food.**
- **If you are able to keep dead trees on your property, these will provide a natural nesting place for Hairy Woodpeckers.**

IN YOUR YARD

The Downy Woodpecker and the Hairy Woodpecker can be distinguished by size difference and length of the bills; the Hairy Woodpecker has the longer bill. Binoculars will show the all-white outer tail feathers of the Hairy Woodpecker compared to the black-spotted outer tail feathers of the Downy Woodpecker.

House Finch
Haemorhous mexicanus

Male and female

GENERAL INFORMATION

- **Male:** A small bird with brownish back, raspberry-red wash on head and belly with brown streaking.
- **Female:** A small brown-streaked bird with conical bill.
- **Range:** Found in all of the US except the extreme southern portions of the Gulf states.
- **Migration:** Found year-round in its range.
- **Preferred Food:** Millet, Nyjer seed, sunflower seed.
- **Preferred Feeders:** Ground forager, Nyjer feeder, tube feeder.
- **Nesting:**
    - **Natural:** A cup-shaped nest made from natural materials and placed in conifers or in parts of buildings.
    - **Man-made:** Will not nest in man-made structures.

- **Eggs:** Light blue with sparse blackish spotting, approximately ¾" long.

TIPS FOR ATTRACTING

- **Providing sunflower seed and Nyjer seed in your feeders will undoubtedly attract the very common House Finch.**
- **Clean your feeders every two weeks to prevent spreading of a bacterial infection called House Finch eye disease, which primarily affects House Finches but will spread to other species.**

IN YOUR YARD

The House Finch is sometimes confused with the Purple Finch. The male House Finch has very distinct streaking on the head and lower body, with raspberry coloring. The Purple Finch has more intense coloring overall with no streaking on the sides near the wings. The House Finch was introduced into New York City from its native western North America. Since 1940, it spread westward until it met the western population's range and has become one of the most common birds found in backyards across the country.

House Sparrow
Passer domesticus

Male and female

GENERAL INFORMATION

- **Male:** A small bird with light-gray belly, black throat, and gray forehead, chestnut on the back of the head.
- **Female:** A small bird with a brownish cap, light-gray belly and throat, and light tan eye stripe.
- **Range:** Found throughout the US.
- **Migration:** Found year-round in its range.
- **Preferred Food:** Cracked corn, millet, suet, sunflower seed.
- **Preferred Feeders:** Ground forager, suet feeder, tube feeder.
- **Nesting:**
    - **Natural:** A cavity nest lined with vegetation and man-made materials placed in man-made structures or nest boxes.

- **Man-made:** Providing nest boxes is discouraged.
- **Eggs:** Creamy to olive brown with brown splotching, approximately ⅞" long.

TIPS FOR ATTRACTING

- **This species will most likely be in your backyard whether you choose to place feeders out or not because of its successful adaptation to living with humans.**
- **Any seed type will attract the House Sparrow, and they will eat at feeders or on the ground.**

IN YOUR YARD

The House Sparrow was introduced into North America in 1851 in New York City, and by the early 1900s it had spread across the continent. Much like the European Starling, the House Sparrow is viewed by some as a pest species, although it is a little less gregarious than the starling. Nevertheless, it has displaced many cavity-nesting species with its aggressive breeding site behavior, causing some of those species' populations to fall, including Eastern Bluebirds, Purple Martins, and many others. To limit House Sparrows' visits to your feeders, offer specific food types such as safflower seed and sunflower seed, since the House Sparrow likes the smaller varieties of seeds.

House Wren
Troglodytes aedon

Male and female House Wrens are identical in appearance.

GENERAL INFORMATION

- **Male:** A very small brown bird with light streaking on breast and short, barred tail.
- **Female:** The female House Wren is not visibly different from the male.
- **Range:** Found throughout the US.
- **Migration:** Breeds in the upper two-thirds of the US, winters mostly in Texas, Gulf states, and southern mid-Atlantic.
- **Preferred Food:** Mealworms, millet, suet.
- **Preferred Feeders:** Ground forager, suet feeder, wire mesh (mealworms).
- **Nesting:**
  - **Natural:** A nest in natural cavities or man-made objects with cavities, including flowerpots, shoes, and watering cans.
  - **Man-made:** 5" D × 5" W × 8" H nest box, 1"-diameter hole, placed near shrubs and about 4'–10' off the ground.
- **Eggs:** Light brown with darker brown splotching mainly at one end, approximately ⅝" long.

TIPS FOR ATTRACTING

- **The House Wren is a very common bird in backyards and one that you can get to nest in your backyard with little trouble using household items with a cavity big enough for them to nest in, such as clay pots, shoes, or watering cans.**
- **Wrens like to move about in shrubs, thickets, and brush, so having this type of foliage can entice this species to visit and stay in your yard.**
- **The wren's diet is mostly insectivorous, so having mealworms at your feeders will be a very attractive option for the House Wren, and the vegetation you have will provide natural foraging areas for them.**

IN YOUR YARD

The House Wren is different from other wren species in that it is comfortable feeding higher off the ground; other wrens would rather forage low to the ground. The House Wren's song will become easily identifiable once you have heard it. It is unlike most other birds' songs; its song is a bubbly string of repeated phrases that is sung very frequently. One way of enticing the House Wren to visit your yard is to have multiple, differing sources of water, such as a ground bath, pedestal, or dripping birdbath.

Lesser Goldfinch
Spinus psaltria

Male and female

GENERAL INFORMATION

- **Male:** A small yellow-breasted finch with yellow throat and black cap, dark gray back, black wings and tail, and white wing patch.
- **Female:** A small finch with pale yellow–washed belly, breast, and throat, olive head and back, black wings and tail, and white wing patch.
- **Range:** Found in the West Coast states and the southwestern states.
- **Migration:** Found year-round along the coast states and the extreme Southwest, breeds in more interior parts of its range.
- **Preferred Food:** Millet, Nyjer seed, sunflower seed.
- **Preferred Feeders:** Nyjer feeder, tube feeder.
- **Nesting:**

- **Natural:** A woven cup made from natural fibers and placed in trees or shrubs near moving water.
- **Man-made:** Will not nest in man-made structures.
- **Eggs:** Creamy blue, approximately ⅝" long.

TIPS FOR ATTRACTING

- Providing Nyjer seed and sunflower seed for other finches will bring the Lesser Goldfinch to your backyard.
- Check your Nyjer seed feeders periodically to see if seeds are moldy, wet, or clumping. This type of seed can become rancid, and goldfinches may then avoid going to those feeders until the seed is replenished with a fresh supply.
- Birdbaths and water features are especially needed by Lesser Goldfinches because of their diet and habitat.
- Goldfinches like to feed in groups, so either get more feeders to place around your yard or purchase longer tube feeders with more perches to accommodate the number of birds visiting.

IN YOUR YARD

Lesser Goldfinches can vary in appearance. Individuals found in the West Coast states have greenish backs as illustrated here, while those in the interior states will have black backs. Both goldfinch species mentioned may become less common during nesting time in late summer. They prefer to stay close to their nests and are also foraging for natural seed supplies.

Mourning Dove
Zenaida macroura

Male and female

GENERAL INFORMATION

- **Male:** A larger pinkish-gray dove with a long tail, dark spots on back and wings.
- **Female:** The female Mourning Dove is very similar to the male but body is brownish-gray overall.
- **Range:** Found throughout the US except for the northern Plains states and the Rockies.
- **Migration:** Found year-round in its range.
- **Preferred Food:** Cracked corn, millet, sunflower seed.
- **Preferred Feeders:** Ground forager, hopper feeder, tray feeder.
- **Nesting:**
  - **Natural:** A loose accumulation of natural materials placed in dense shrubs or trees.
  - **Man-made:** A "V" trough 8" L × 2" W × 2" D, 2" × 7" front and 6" × 7" back, placed near trees and about 6'–12' off the ground.

- **Eggs:** White unmarked, approximately 1 ⅛" long.

TIPS FOR ATTRACTING

- Providing a source of food where some will spill to the ground is all you need to bring Mourning Doves to your feeders.
- Conifers or dense thickets will attract Mourning Doves for nesting, and bare spots on the ground provide areas for dust bathing.
- Because it is off the ground, a pedestal birdbath will protect the Mourning Dove while it is drinking and bathing.

IN YOUR YARD

Mourning Doves are widespread across the US and are virtually a guaranteed visitor to your backyard. Their cooing is heard in the early mornings all the way to dusk. They prefer to feed on the ground, so nearby cats do pose a danger to them. Make sure feeding stations are away from shrubbery to allow the doves time to see any approaching predators. Doves feed and then retire to a branch, rooftop, or power line to digest their food, and then return to the feeder.

Northern Cardinal
Cardinalis cardinalis

Male and female

GENERAL INFORMATION

- **Male:** A medium-sized red bird with a crest and black on the chin and face.
- **Female:** A brownish medium-sized bird with red bill and crest, and reddish wings and tail.
- **Range:** Found in the Plains states eastward.
- **Migration:** Found year-round in its range.
- **Preferred Food:** Cracked corn, mealworms, peanut hearts, safflower seed, sunflower seed.
- **Preferred Feeders:** Ground forager, tray feeder, tube feeder, wire mesh (mealworms, peanut hearts).
- **Nesting:**
  - **Natural:** A multilayered nest made with different natural materials.
  - **Man-made:** Will not nest in man-made structures.

- **Eggs:** Bluish-tan with light brown spotting, approximately 1" long.

TIPS FOR ATTRACTING

- **Berry-producing shrubs and trees can provide natural food and nesting opportunities for Northern Cardinals in your yard.**
- **Shelled sunflower and safflower seeds are a must if you are trying to attract cardinals to your backyard feeders.**
- **Since cardinals are year-round feeder visitors, a heated birdbath may be too hard to resist in the cold of winter.**

IN YOUR YARD

Northern Cardinals are probably one of the most easily identifiable birds in eastern North America, with all-red bodies and crest. They keep the same plumage year-round and present a striking contrast in winter against brown branches and white snow. Their songs are distinct and can be memorized after hearing them a few times. Roughly 30 percent of the cardinal's diet is insects, many of which are pest species; for those who garden, this is an additional benefit.

Northern Flicker
Colaptes auratus

Male and female

GENERAL INFORMATION

- **Male:** A larger woodpecker with spotted breast, black band on chest, black mustache, red on the back of the head, and white rump patch shown when flying.
- **Female:** The female is very similar to the male but lacks the black mustache.
- **Range:** Found in all the US.
- **Migration:** Found year-round in most of range, summer movement to northern Plains and New England states, winter movement to Texas, southern California, and Arizona.
- **Preferred Food:** Cracked corn, peanuts, peanut hearts, suet, sunflower seed.
- **Preferred Feeders:** Ground forager, suet feeder, tray feeder, tube feeder, wire mesh (peanuts, peanut hearts).
- **Nesting:**
  - **Natural:** A cavity nest found in a dead tree or dead branch.

- **Man-made:** 7" D × 7" W × 24" D nest box, 2 ½"-diameter hole, placed on tree 6'–20' off the ground, lined with wood shavings.
- **Eggs:** Unmarked white, approximately 1 ⅛" long.

TIPS FOR ATTRACTING

- **Unlike other woodpeckers, flickers may occasionally visit feeders and birdbaths while in your yard looking for insects on the ground or in trees.**
- **Planting fruit-producing trees and shrubs will provide food for flickers in the winter when insects are harder to find.**
- **If you live in the northern part of range, the Northern Flicker may be absent from your feeders when they migrate southward in winter.**

IN YOUR YARD

The Northern Flicker is the only woodpecker to forage on the ground and will be seen there as much as in a tree, consuming ants in large quantities. There are two geographic races in the US. Illustrated here is the "yellow-shafted" race, which is found in the eastern US. The "red-shafted" race is found in the western US and will flash red instead of yellow. Also, the "red-shafted" male has a red mustache and lacks the red on the back of the head.

Northern Mockingbird
Mimus polyglottos

Male and female Northern Mockingbirds are identical in appearance.

GENERAL INFORMATION

- **Male:** A larger white-bellied and gray-backed bird with long black tail showing white wing patches and outer tail feathers in flight.
- **Female:** The female Northern Mockingbird is not visibly different from the male.
- **Range:** Found in the southwestern half of the US and all over the eastern half except upper New England.
- **Migration:** Found year-round in most of its range, breeding in the northern sections.
- **Preferred Food:** Fruit, suet, sunflower seed.
- **Preferred Feeders:** Ground forager, fruit/jelly feeder, suet feeder.
- **Nesting:**
  - **Natural:** A cuplike nest made of twigs and lined with natural and man-made materials.
  - **Man-made:** Will not nest in man-made structures.
- **Eggs:** Light blue with light brown splotching, approximately 1" long.

TIPS FOR ATTRACTING

- Like its cousins the Gray Catbird and the Brown Thrasher, the Northern Mockingbird is at home in the thickets and dense brush. Having plantings like this will attract the mockingbird to your backyard.
- The mockingbird will visit yards with open areas for ground foraging and for bathing at a birdbath, but feeder visits may not be frequent.
- In its range, the Northern Mockingbird can be found in urban settings as well as rural, making it an exciting and beautiful visitor to a city backyard.

IN YOUR YARD

The Northern Mockingbird is the "bird of a thousand voices," mimicking many other birds and even human-produced sounds. The sounds are usually repeated two or three times each, before the bird moves on to another call or song, which is again repeated. Mockingbirds usually select singing locations on the ground or on easily visible perching areas in shrubs and trees. The white flashing in the wings and tail make identification relatively easy.

Pileated Woodpecker
Dryocopus pileatus

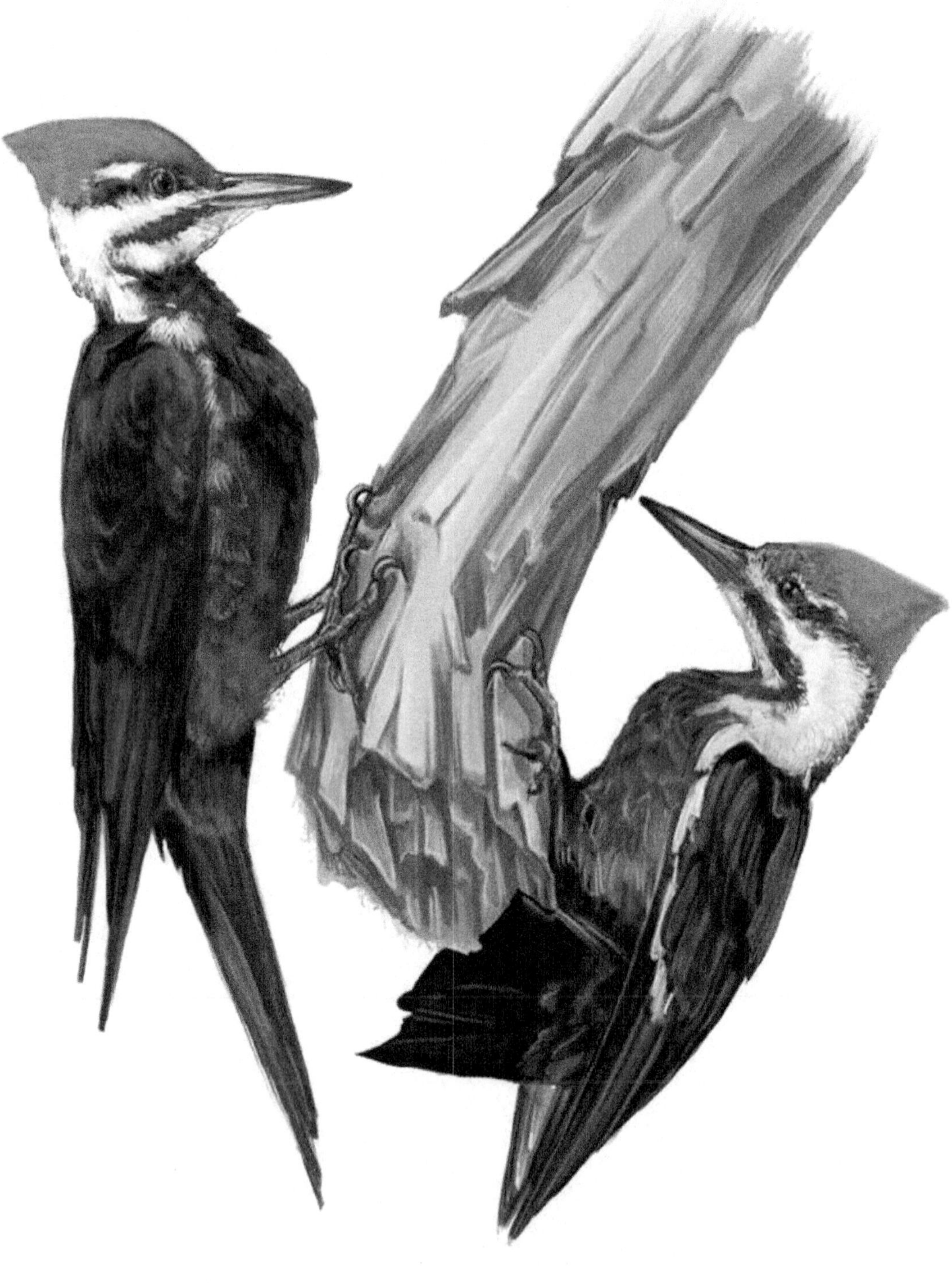

Male and female

GENERAL INFORMATION

- **Male:** A very large woodpecker with black body, white striping on face, and red from bill back to tip of crest, showing white wing patches in flight.
- **Female:** The female is very similar to the male except that it has a black forehead and red only on the crest.
- **Range:** Found east of the Great Plains and the northwestern coastal states.
- **Migration:** Found year-round in its range.
- **Preferred Food:** Peanuts, suet, sunflower seed.
- **Preferred Feeders:** Suet feeder, wire mesh (peanuts).
- **Nesting:**
  - **Natural:** A cavity nest found in a large dead tree or dead branch.
  - **Man-made:** Will not nest in man-made structures.
- **Eggs:** Unmarked white, approximately 1 ⅜" long.

TIPS FOR ATTRACTING

- **Suet feeders should be large enough to hold the Pileated Woodpecker or be placed on the trunk of a tree where the birds can support themselves.**
- **For those with larger acreage, consider leaving dead trees standing for Pileated Woodpecker breeding pairs to excavate a cavity for nesting.**

IN YOUR YARD

North America's largest woodpecker is truly one of the most magnificent birds to visit your backyard, and its sheer size will have you running for your camera. Pileated Woodpeckers live in mature forests, so your proximity to a wooded area will be key to having them visit your backyard. If one comes to your yard, remember they are not as comfortable as other woodpecker species around humans and will take flight quickly.

Pine Siskin
Spinus pinus

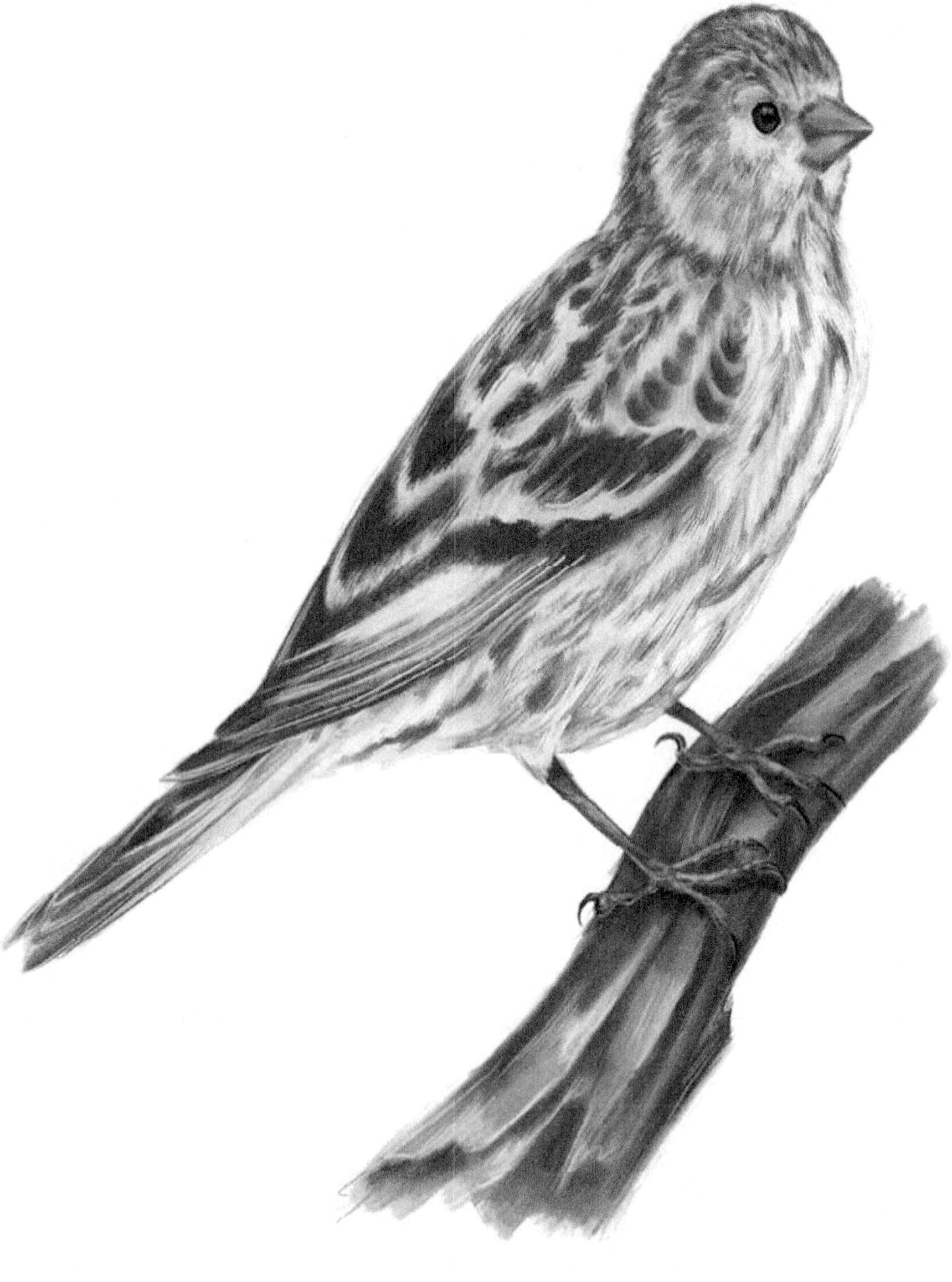

Male and female Pine Siskins are identical in appearance.

GENERAL INFORMATION

- **Male:** A small brown-streaked finch with yellow wash on the wings, base of tail, and outer tail feathers.
- **Female:** The female Pine Siskin is not visibly different from the male.
- **Range:** Found in all of the US except for the extreme Gulf states.
- **Migration:** Winters in most of the US range except for breeding in the Northwest, Rockies, and upper Great Lakes area.
- **Preferred Food:** Millet, Nyjer seed, peanut hearts, sunflower seed.
- **Preferred Feeders:** Nyjer feeder, tray feeder, tube feeder, wire mesh (peanut hearts).
- **Nesting:**
  - **Natural:** A shallow woven bowl made of natural materials.
  - **Man-made:** Will not nest in man-made structures.
- **Eggs:** Creamy blue with sparse spotting, approximately ¾" long.

TIPS FOR ATTRACTING

- **When Pine Siskins show up, they travel in relatively large flocks, looking for Nyjer seed and hulled sunflower seed in particular.**
- **Siskins prefer somewhat forested areas opening up into clearings, especially if cone-bearing trees are nearby.**
- **The presence of siskins can fluctuate each year; they can visit your feeder this year and then be absent the next, due to seed crop quantities in the area. They are nomadic in order to find natural food sources.**

IN YOUR YARD

Pine Siskins have been on the decline in recent years, perhaps due to diminishing nesting habitat, predation of its young, and susceptibility to *Salmonella* infection from feeders not routinely cleaned. If siskins are present in your area, please take the time to clean feeders at least twice a month to prevent an avian outbreak. Providing a heated birdbath in cold weather will be an added attraction to flocks of Pine Siskins.

Pine Warbler
Setophaga pinus

Male and female

GENERAL INFORMATION

- **Male:** A small warbler with yellow breast and throat, greenish head and back, white belly with dark wings and two white wing bars.
- **Female:** The female Pine Warbler is similar to the male but with duller coloring.
- **Range:** Found in the eastern third of the US.
- **Migration:** Breeds in the upper half of range, year-round in the southern half, winters in Texas and the lower Gulf states.
- **Preferred Food:** Fruit, mealworms, suet.
- **Preferred Feeders:** Fruit/jelly feeder, suet feeder, wire mesh (fruit, mealworms).
- **Nesting:**
  - **Natural:** A small cuplike nest made with natural materials and spider silk.
  - **Man-made:** Will not nest in man-made structures.
- **Eggs:** Creamy with brown splotches, approximately ¾" long.

TIPS FOR ATTRACTING

- **Pine Warblers will feed on suet during the winter season when their natural diet of insects is lacking.**
- **Pine cones covered with peanut butter and seed, especially sunflower, will attract Pine Warblers and other suet eaters.**
- **As its name implies, the Pine Warbler spends a lot of its time in pine trees, so planting a grove of these may attract this species when the trees mature.**

IN YOUR YARD

The Pine Warbler is one of the few warblers that will frequent feeders, although others may forage in trees during migration. This species and the Yellow-rumped Warbler are both suet eaters, so both may visit the suet feeder in your backyard. Pine Warblers are also insect eaters, so you might want to place mealworms in a mesh feeder to check the attractiveness of this food source.

Purple Finch
Haemorhous purpureus

Male and female

GENERAL INFORMATION

- **Male:** A small finch with heavy raspberry-red wash on head, back, throat, and belly.
- **Female:** The female Purple Finch is heavily streaked on the belly and breast, with thick bill, creamy eye stripe, and darker face patch.
- **Range:** Found along the West Coast and the eastern half of the US except the Gulf states.
- **Migration:** Found year-round on the West Coast, New England, and upper Great Lakes, winters in the Plains states and the southern US.
- **Preferred Food:** Millet, Nyjer seed, peanut hearts, sunflower seed.
- **Preferred Feeders:** Nyjer feeder, tray feeder, tube feeder, wire mesh (peanut hearts).
- **Nesting:**
  - **Natural:** A cuplike nest made with natural materials.

- **Man-made:** Will not nest in man-made structures.
- **Eggs:** Light blue with sparse blackish spotting, approximately ⅞" long.

TIPS FOR ATTRACTING

- **Black oil sunflower seed is your best bet in attracting Purple Finches if you live in their range and habitat.**
- **Coniferous trees and fruit-bearing shrubs and trees will make your yard more appealing to visits by this finch.**
- **For most of the US, the Purple Finch is a winter backyard visitor, so be sure to have its favorite foods out beginning in late fall if you don't have feeders out all year.**

IN YOUR YARD

There often is confusion about whether House Finches or Purple Finches are visiting your feeders. If the bird has streaking on its sides and the coloring of the head is mixed with brown, then you have a House Finch. Purple Finches are more often found in open areas in the country versus the suburbs and cities. This is due in part to competition between the House Finch and the Purple Finch. The populations of the latter have been declining since the House Finch was introduced on the East Coast in the 1950s. In its winter range, it can be present one year and then absent for several in periodic patterns called irruptions.

Purple Martin
Progne subis

Male and female

GENERAL INFORMATION

- **Male:** A violet-blue medium-sized bird with blackish wings.
- **Female:** The female Purple Martin is dark overall with paler belly.
- **Range:** Found in the Plains states eastward, local areas in the west.
- **Migration:** Breeds in its range, winters outside the US.
- **Preferred Food:** Airborne insects.
- **Preferred Feeders:** Will not come to feeders.
- **Nesting:**
  - **Natural:** Cavity nester in trees or cactus along with man-made structures.
  - **Man-made:** A commercially made colony house attached to a pole at least 60' from trees or structures, 15'–20' off the ground.
- **Eggs:** White unmarked, approximately ⅞" long.

TIPS FOR ATTRACTING

- **The primary way to get Purple Martins to your backyard is to mount Purple Martin houses on poles if you live in their range and habitat.**
- **Purple Martins may nest in pairs, but they often nest communally in houses designed for up to twenty or more nesting pairs.**
- **The Purple Martin house is susceptible to habitation by House Sparrows and European Starlings. If you are serious about having Purple Martins nesting in your backyard, you will need to periodically remove nests from these pest species from the Purple Martin houses.**

IN YOUR YARD

In the fall, Purple Martins will gather in large flocks along with swallows to begin their southward migration to South America. Purple Martins avoid competition with swallows by flying more than 150' above the ground eating flying insects. They are very beneficial for gardening due to their diet of insects. The populations of Purple Martins have declined since the 1960s mostly due to competition with cavity-nesting species like the House Sparrow and the European Starling, which are more aggressive at their nest sites.

Red-bellied Woodpecker
Melanerpes carolinus

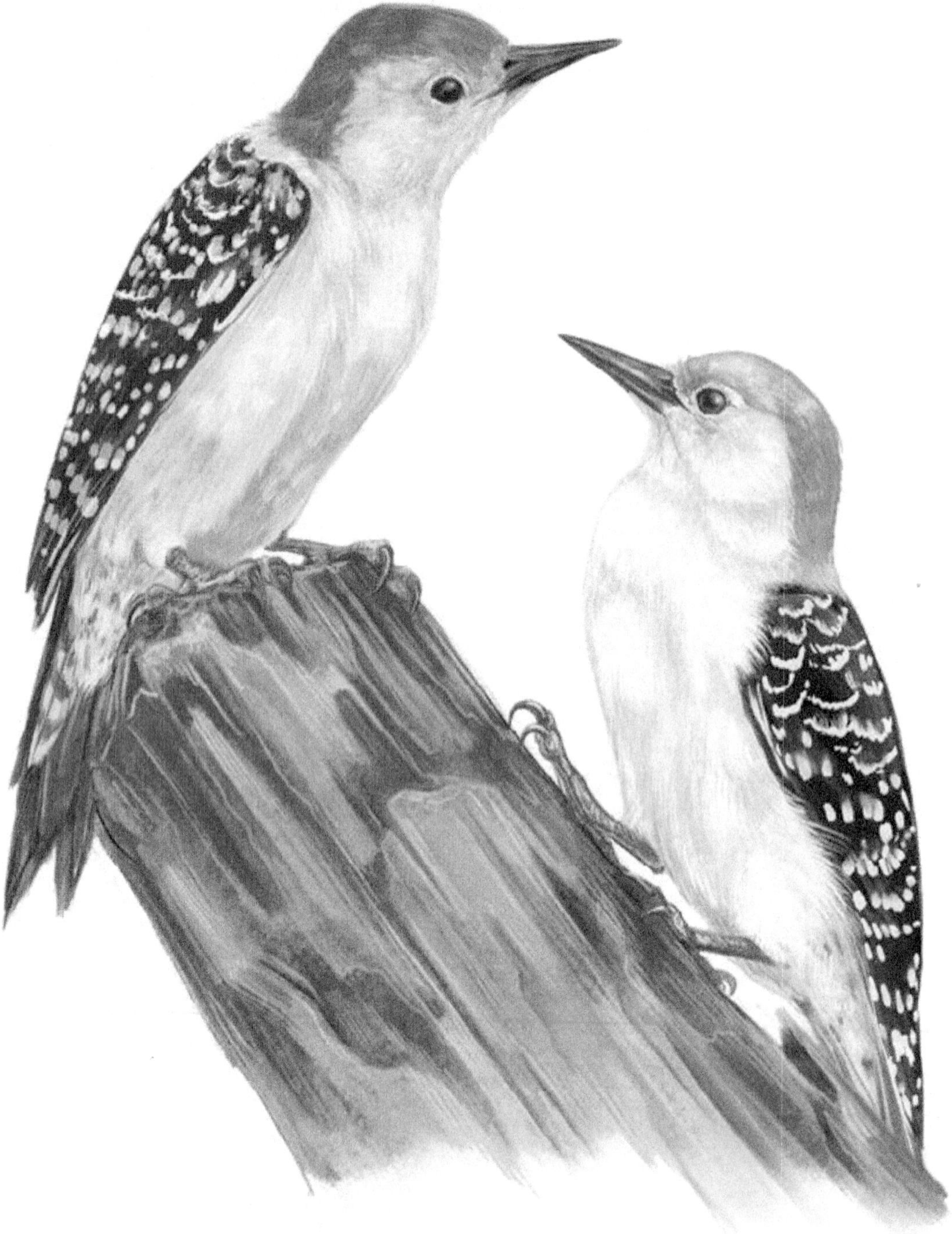

Male and female

GENERAL INFORMATION

- **Male:** A medium-sized woodpecker with black-and-white-striped back, white breast with pinkish belly, and red from forehead to back of the head.
- **Female:** The female is very similar to the male but is lacking red on the forehead.
- **Range:** Found in all of the eastern states and the eastern Plains states.
- **Migration:** Found year-round in its range.
- **Preferred Food:** Peanuts, suet, sunflower seed.
- **Preferred Feeders:** Suet feeder, tube feeder, wire mesh (peanuts).
- **Nesting:**
  - **Natural:** A cavity nest found in dead trees or branches, which it will excavate.
  - **Man-made:** Will not nest in man-made structures.
- **Eggs:** White unmarked, approximately ¾" long.

TIPS FOR ATTRACTING

- **The Red-bellied Woodpecker is a common species in rural and suburban areas of the eastern US and will visit tray, suet, and tube feeders quite often, as well as forage for insects on trees.**
- **Red-bellied Woodpeckers love to eat suet and peanuts in the shell, so be sure to have these feeders out for this species.**

IN YOUR YARD

Red-bellied Woodpeckers can be a little forceful when they visit feeders, sometimes pushing other birds away temporarily while they feed. If you have oak or beech trees on your property you may be in luck, because these woodpeckers have been observed eating acorns and beechnuts along with some fruits from trees and shrubs. They do have a red belly, but you will need to see them at a feeder and be at the correct angle to see the pink-red patch.

Red-breasted Nuthatch
Sitta canadensis

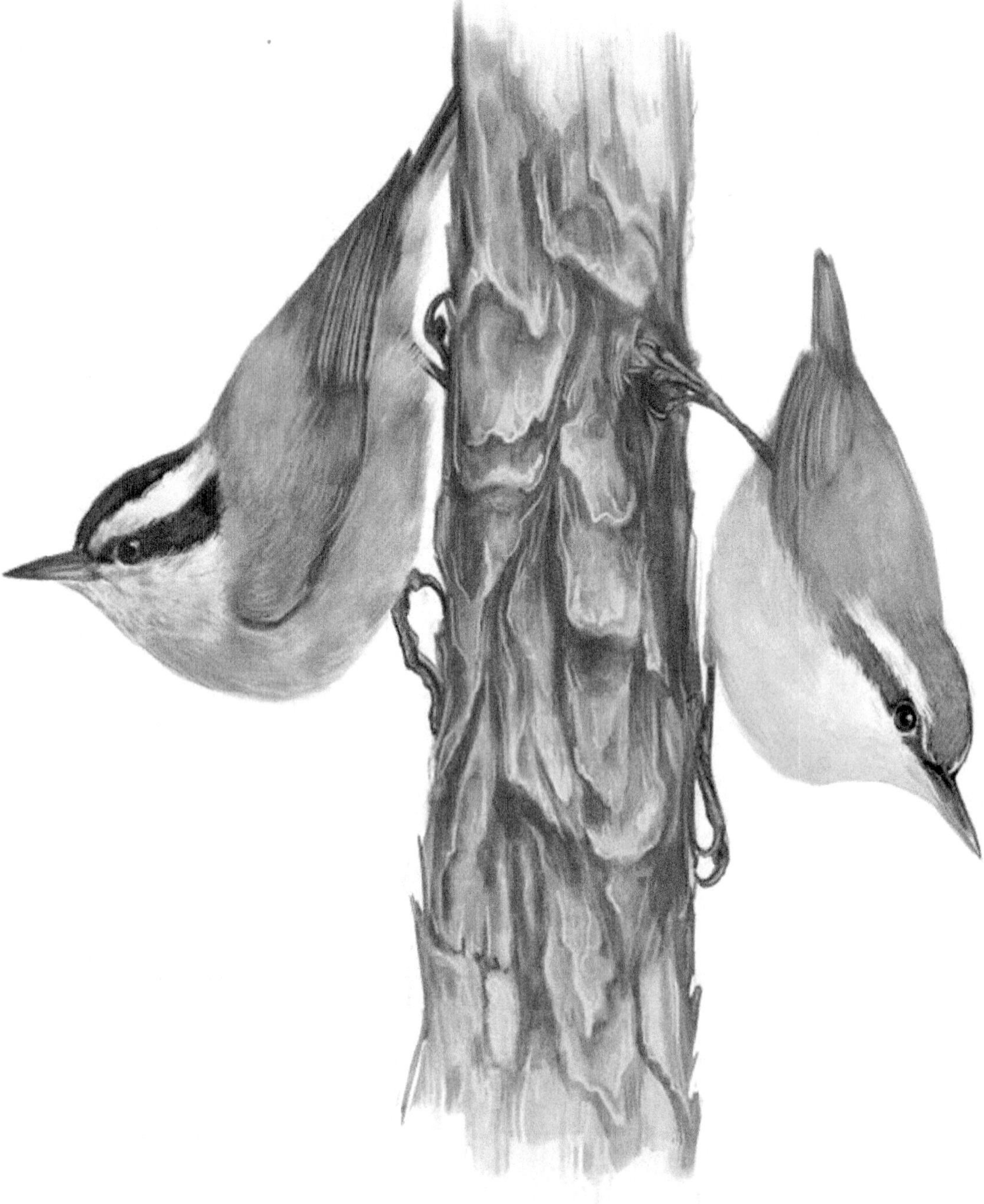

Male and female

GENERAL INFORMATION

- **Male:** A small blue-gray-backed bird with orange belly and black eye stripe.
- **Female:** The female is very similar to the male Red-breasted Nuthatch but duller.
- **Range:** Found in most of the US except Florida.
- **Migration:** Found year-round in the Rockies, New England, and the upper Great Lakes, winters elsewhere in its range.
- **Preferred Food:** Peanuts, peanut butter, suet, sunflower seed.
- **Preferred Feeders:** Hopper feeder, suet feeder, tray feeder, tube feeder, wire mesh (peanuts).
- **Nesting:**
  - **Natural:** A cavity nest found in trees lined with natural materials.
  - **Man-made:** 5" D × 5" W × 8" H nest box, 1 ¼"-diameter hole, placed 5'–15' off the ground.
- **Eggs:** Creamy with brown splotches, approximately ⅝" long.

TIPS FOR ATTRACTING

- **The Red-breasted Nuthatch will be a frequent flyer at your feeders as long as you provide its favorite foods, especially sunflower seed and suet.**
- **The nuthatch is a quick but regular visitor to your feeders. It likes to consume the seed elsewhere and usually flies off to a tree to eat or cache away its find.**
- **The Red-breasted Nuthatch can be timid around larger birds. Having feeders with cages or without perches to minimize the number of birds at those feeders may give the nuthatch a more comfortable place to feed.**

IN YOUR YARD

One of the cute little birds that will grab a seed or two and then fly off to eat, the Red-breasted Nuthatch is a backyard favorite. If they happen to nest in a box you provided, be aware that they typically place pitch from a conifer around the nest box opening as a way to deter predators or keep insects away from their young.

Red-winged Blackbird
Agelaius phoeniceus

Male and female

GENERAL INFORMATION

- **Male:** A medium-sized black bird with red and yellow patch on the shoulder.
- **Female:** A medium-sized heavily streaked brown bird with darker face patch.
- **Range:** Found throughout most of the US.
- **Migration:** Found year-round in most of its range, migrates into the northernmost states for breeding.
- **Preferred Food:** Cracked corn, suet, sunflower seed.
- **Preferred Feeders:** Ground forager, hopper feeder, tray feeder, tube feeder.
- **Nesting:**
  - **Natural:** A nest woven with natural materials into vertical vegetation in marshy areas.
  - **Man-made:** Will not nest in man-made structures.
- **Eggs:** Light blue with brown swirling, approximately 1" long.

TIPS FOR ATTRACTING

- A very common bird in its range, the Red-winged Blackbird will be a common visitor to your backyard as long as there is some food on the ground.
- If you don't want the Red-winged Blackbird at your feeders, place cages around tube feeders or offer foods that are less appealing to this species.
- Another option is to place a ground tray feeder or food directly on the ground in a location away from other feeders to draw Red-winged Blackbirds away from feeders but still attract them to your yard.

IN YOUR YARD

Like most of the other blackbirds, the Red-winged Blackbird can be slightly assertive when at feeders and may cause some birds to temporarily leave a feeder. In winter, large flocks can be found visiting feeders and then quickly disappearing. For those in the northern part of its range, its call is a welcome sign of spring; it is usually one of the very first migrants to start moving northward.

Rose-breasted Grosbeak
Pheucticus ludovicianus

Male and female

GENERAL INFORMATION

- **Male:** A uniquely patterned bird with black head and back, white belly, and rose-red triangular patch on the breast.
- **Female:** A medium-sized brown-streaked bird with heavy bill, dark face patch, and white eye stripe.
- **Range:** Found in the Plains states and eastward.
- **Migration:** Breeds in the upper half of its range, migrates through the lower half of its range.
- **Preferred Food:** Cracked corn, fruit, mealworms, peanuts, safflower seed, sunflower seed.
- **Preferred Feeders:** Fruit/jelly feeder, tube feeder, wire mesh (mealworms, peanuts).
- **Nesting:**

- **Natural:** A loose cuplike nest made from twigs and lined with natural materials, usually in a fork of a tree branch.
- **Man-made:** Will not nest in man-made structures.
- **Eggs:** Greenish-blue with brown splotching, approximately 1" long.

TIPS FOR ATTRACTING

- **The two main ways to attract the Rose-breasted Grosbeak is to provide preferred foods and have fruit-bearing trees and shrubs, including wild grape, hawthorn, dogwood, elderberry, Virginia creeper, and mulberry.**
- **The grosbeak really loves water features, so having multiple birdbaths, perhaps with drippers or misters, may entice more frequent visits.**
- **If you are not in the breeding range, make sure your yard is ready for a migratory stop, perhaps lasting a week or two.**

IN YOUR YARD

The Rose-breasted Grosbeak is a simple-colored bird, but it is beautiful to see. Its song has been described as a robin's with voice lessons, and when you hear it be sure to look at the treetops. It will come to feeders; however, about half of its diet is insects, many of which are insect pests. This makes it a very beneficial visitor, especially if you have a vegetable garden.

Ruby-throated Hummingbird
Archilochus colubris

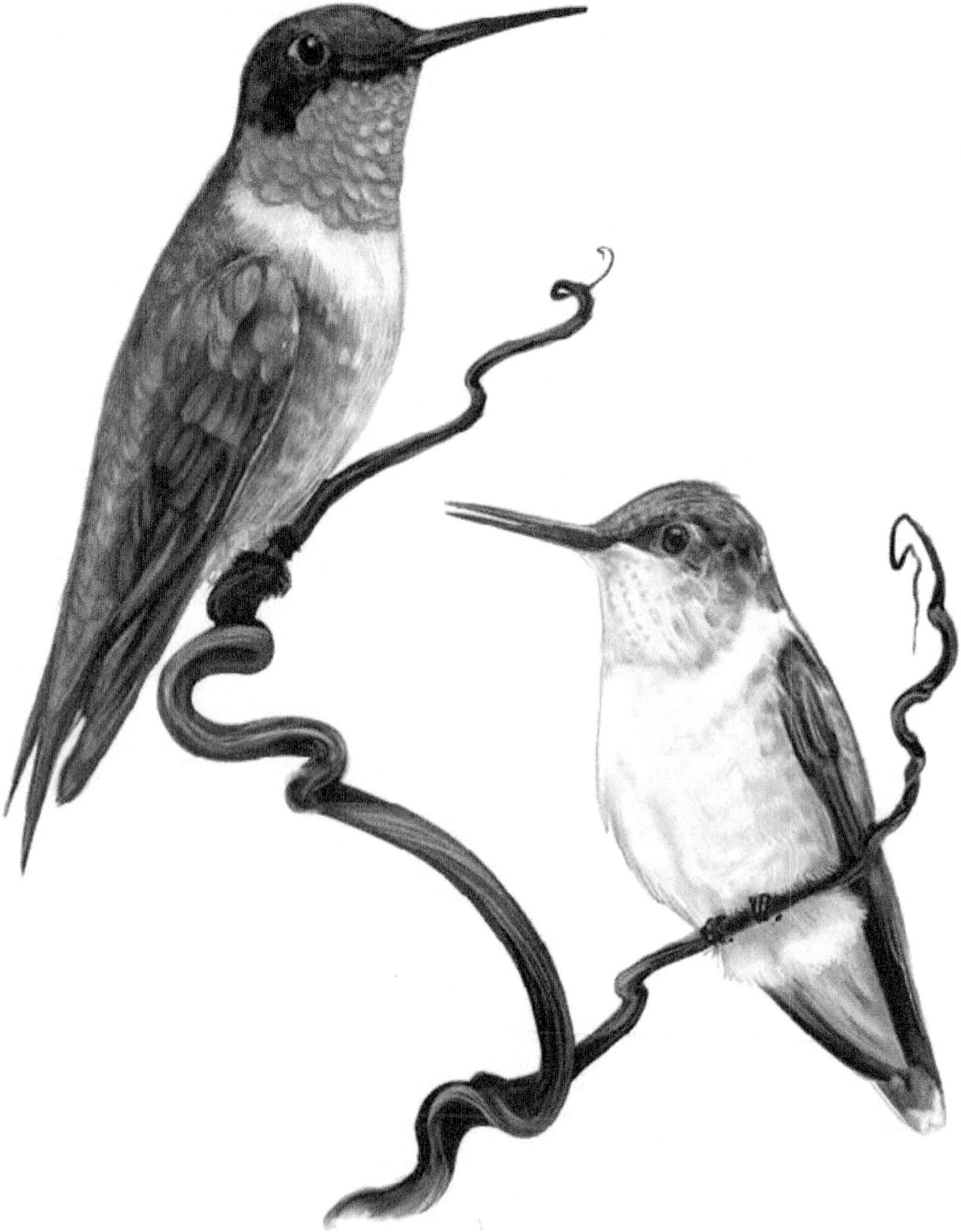

Male and female

GENERAL INFORMATION

- **Male:** A tiny bird with greenish back and belly, white chest, ruby-colored throat.
- **Female:** A tiny bird with greenish back and whitish belly.
- **Range:** Found in the Plains and eastern states.
- **Migration:** Found year-round in the southeastern coasts, breeds in the eastern states, migrates through the Plains states.
- **Preferred Food:** Nectar, flower nectar.
- **Preferred Feeders:** Nectar feeder.
- **Nesting:**
  - **Natural:** A tiny nest of seed fibers and spider silk about 2" across made on top of a small tree branch.
  - **Man-made:** Will not nest in man-made structures.
- **Eggs:** Unmarked white, approximately ½" long.

TIPS FOR ATTRACTING

- Placing nectar feeders near flowering plants may make it easier for the hummingbird to find. It may take several days for a hummingbird to find a newly placed feeder.
- Plant flowers that are favorites of the Ruby-throated Hummingbird, such as columbines, lobelia, and bee balm.
- For those wanting to plant shrubs, check out the butterfly bush, trumpet vine, and honeysuckle.

IN YOUR YARD

The Ruby-throated Hummingbird is the only breeding hummingbird in the eastern US, making this a special visitor for those in that part of the country. No matter how many times you have seen a hummingbird, it is still a special sight to see. Consistently keeping the feeder clean and the nectar fresh guarantees that the Ruby-throated Hummingbird will visit your backyard sanctuary. Be sure to watch for the courtship flight of the male, which makes pendulum-like sweeps in front of the female near shrubs or trees.

Song Sparrow
Melospiza melodia

Male and female Song Sparrows are identical in appearance.

GENERAL INFORMATION

- **Male:** A small brown sparrow with a streaked breast with a central darker spot.
- **Female:** The female Song Sparrow is not visibly different from the male.
- **Range:** Found throughout the US.
- **Migration:** Winters in the lower half of the US, breeds in the northern Plains states, year-round in the rest of its range.
- **Preferred Food:** Cracked corn, millet, sunflower seed.
- **Preferred Feeders:** Ground forager.
- **Nesting:**
  - **Natural:** A small cuplike nest made of natural fibers usually hidden in grass or weeds near the ground.
  - **Man-made:** Will not nest in man-made structures.

- **Eggs:** Light blue with brownish splotching, approximately ⅞" long.

TIPS FOR ATTRACTING

- **The Song Sparrow will surely visit your backyard, given its range, comfort level around people, and the wide variety of food it prefers.**
- **Planting brambles, such as blackberries and raspberries, and mulberry and cherry trees will attract the Song Sparrow to natural food sources.**
- **Listen for the Song Sparrow's frequently voiced song and look for it lurking around on the ground near shrubs and brush piles.**

IN YOUR YARD

The Song Sparrow is one of the most common sparrows in North America. Be sure to look at the Song Sparrow closely and remember what it looks like. There are many other streaked sparrows, and knowing what the Song Sparrow looks like will help you to distinguish it from several other sparrows. There could be some confusion between the Song Sparrow and the Fox Sparrow. The Fox Sparrow is larger and much more rusty-colored than the brown Song Sparrow.

Spotted Towhee
Pipilo maculatus

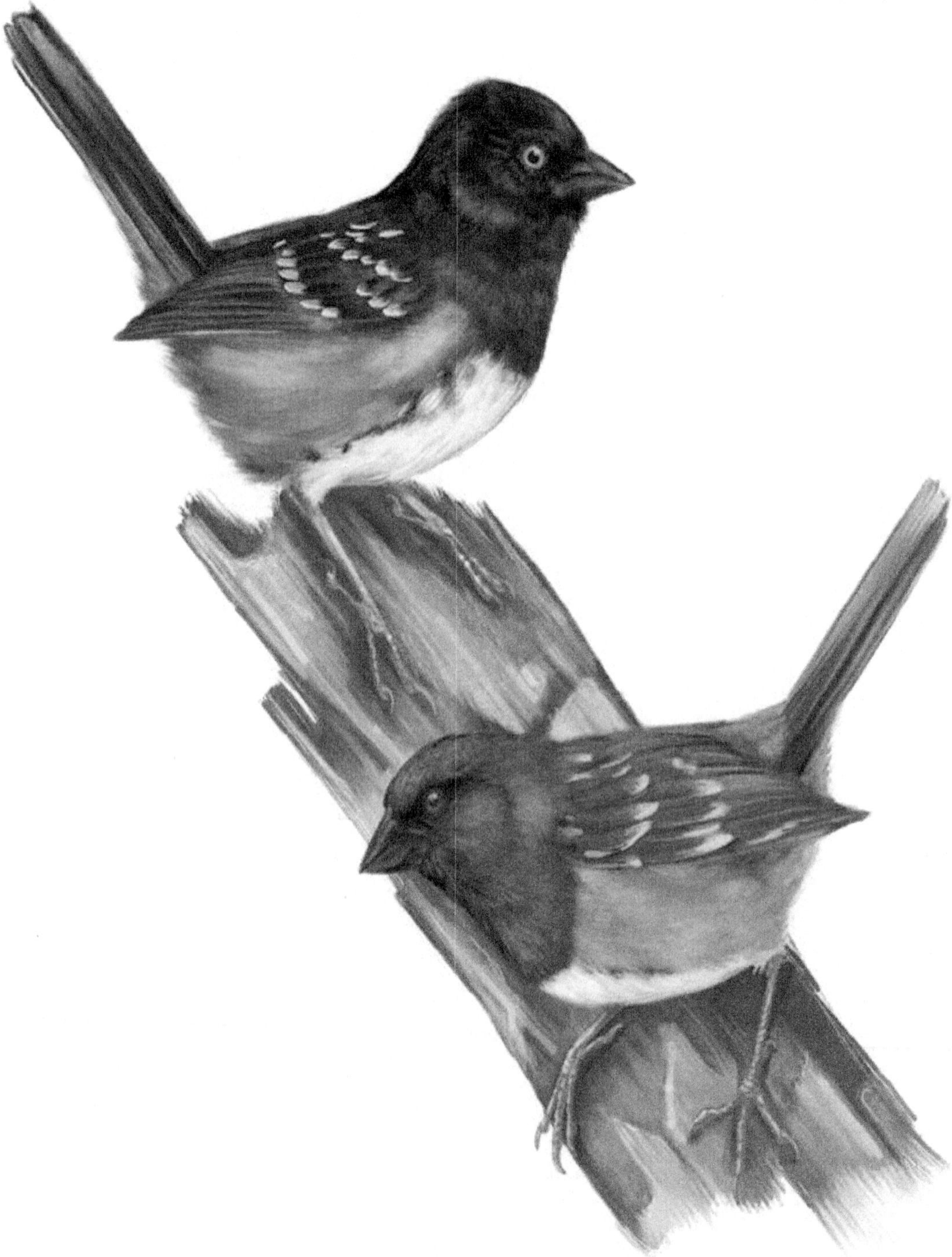

Male and female

GENERAL INFORMATION

- **Male:** This medium-sized bird has a white belly; rusty sides; and a black throat, head, tail, and back with white spots.
- **Female:** The female Spotted Towhee is similar to the male but duller in color.
- **Range:** Found from the Plains states and westward.
- **Migration:** Found year-round on the West Coast and the southwestern states, breeds in the upper Rockies and Plains states, winters in the lower Plains states and Texas.
- **Preferred Food:** Cracked corn, millet, sunflower seed.
- **Preferred Feeders:** Ground forager.
- **Nesting:**
  - **Natural:** A cuplike nest made of bark, twigs, and leaves lined with finer materials built in the thickets, usually hidden against a natural object on the ground.
  - **Man-made:** Will not nest in man-made structures.
- **Eggs:** Creamy with reddish-brown splotches at wider end, approximately ⅞" long.

TIPS FOR ATTRACTING

- Having dense hedges, thickets, and brambles with leaf litter for the Spotted Towhee to feed in will be key to having this species in your yard.
- Plantings that have fruits or berries will attract the Spotted Towhee in the autumn and winter.
- The Spotted Towhee is usually heard singing, scratching at the ground, or overturning leaves to find food before it is seen, so keep your ears alert for these sounds.

IN YOUR YARD

For those in the eastern part of the country, you may come across the related Eastern Towhee (*Pipilo erythrophthalmus*). It is very similar to the Spotted Towhee except it has a solid black back with no white spots. Both species stay near or on the ground when foraging, so be sure to look in places low to the ground when trying to spot one. Due to their leaf-scratching feeding strategy and amount of time on the ground, they are susceptible to predation by cats. If you have towhees and cats, be aware of this fact and perhaps attach a bell to the cat for warning purposes.

Tufted Titmouse
Baeolophus bicolor

Male and female Tufted Titmice are identical in appearance.

GENERAL INFORMATION

- **Male:** A small dark gray bird with a crest, lighter belly, and rusty sides.
- **Female:** The female Tufted Titmouse is not visibly different from the male.
- **Range:** Found east of the Plains states.
- **Migration:** Found year-round in its range.
- **Preferred Food:** Peanuts, peanut hearts, suet, sunflower seed.
- **Preferred Feeders:** Suet feeder, tray feeder, tube feeder, wire mesh (peanuts).
- **Nesting:**
  - **Natural:** A cavity nest found inside a previously excavated hole, usually lined with animal hairs.
  - **Man-made:** 5" D × 5" W × 8" H nest box, 1 ¼"-diameter hole, placed in partial shade about 5'–15' off the ground.
- **Eggs:** Creamy with brownish splotching heavier at wider end, approximately ¾" long.

TIPS FOR ATTRACTING

- Tufted Titmice are a very common backyard bird given the right habitat conditions and food provided at your feeders.
- Providing nest boxes greatly increases your chances for keeping the bird in your yard since they are cavity nesters but cannot excavate their own cavities.
- As with many of the other birds discussed, it is recommended that you plant fruit-bearing trees and shrubs, such as oaks, serviceberry, mulberry, and brambles, as these will draw the titmouse in for foraging.

IN YOUR YARD

The Tufted Titmouse will often forage with chickadees, nuthatches, and kinglets in the autumn and winter seasons. The Titmouse is one species that will cache some of the seeds taken from feeders into crevices in tree bark. Their calls of "peter, peter, peter" are a giveaway to their presence, but they can still be hard to spot. They are a favorite bird of gardeners because of the large number of insects eaten as part of their diet.

Varied Thrush
Ixoreus naevius

Male and female

GENERAL INFORMATION

- **Male:** A larger slate-gray bird with orange belly and throat, black chest band, orange eye stripe, and patterning in the wing.
- **Female:** The female is very similar to the male but duller and with a gray partial chest band.
- **Range:** Found in the West Coast states.
- **Migration:** Winters into the interior West Coast states.
- **Preferred Food:** Fruit and berries, mealworms, suet.
- **Preferred Feeders:** Fruit/jelly feeder, suet feeder, wire mesh (mealworms).
- **Nesting:**
  - **Natural:** A nest made of twigs, lined with moss and mud, then lined with finer natural materials, built in the understory of mature woods.
  - **Man-made:** Will not nest in man-made structures.

- **Eggs:** Light blue with some brownish spotting, approximately 1 ¼" long.

TIPS FOR ATTRACTING

- **The Varied Thrush will most likely be a fall and winter visitor, taking advantage of any fruiting trees and shrubs in your yard.**
- **This thrush is an insect eater during nesting times, and mealworms may be a great food source for nestlings if you are trying to attract a Varied Thrush to your backyard.**
- **The Varied Thrush is also a ground forager and sometimes consumes sunflower seed spread on the ground.**

IN YOUR YARD

Even though Varied Thrushes won't visit most feeders, they do forage on the ground for worms, insects, and other arthropods in lawns. Loss of mature forest acreage has reduced nesting areas, and this thrush is in decline. Since this thrush is very frequently on the ground, it is also a victim of cats. Consider placing a bell on cats to help maintain the Varied Thrush population near you.

White-breasted Nuthatch
Sitta carolinensis

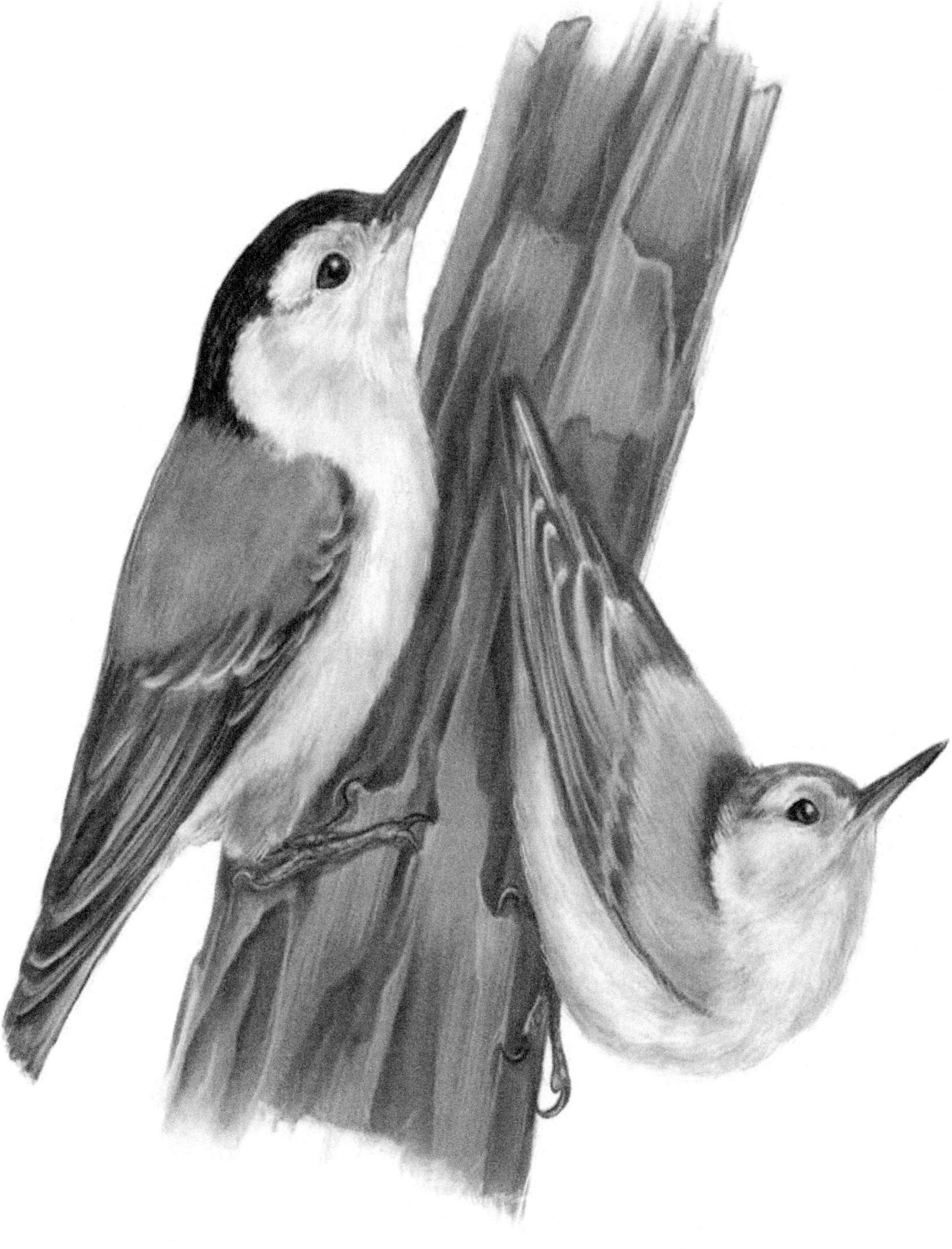

Male and female

GENERAL INFORMATION

- **Male:** A small white bird with white breast and belly, blue-gray back, and black cap.
- **Female:** The female is similar to the male but its cap is blue-gray, not black.
- **Range:** Found in all of the US except for Texas, the Gulf states, and some northwestern regions.
- **Migration:** Found year-round in its range.
- **Preferred Food:** Peanuts, peanut hearts, suet, sunflower seed.
- **Preferred Feeders:** Hopper feeder, suet feeder, tray feeder, tube feeder.
- **Nesting:**
    - **Natural:** A cavity nest in a previously used cavity, lined on the bottom with coarser natural materials and then lined with feathers and grasses.
    - **Man-made:** 5" D × 5" W × 8" H nest box, 1 ¼"-diameter hole, placed 5'–20' off the ground.
- **Eggs:** Creamy with brownish splotching heavier at wider end, approximately ¾" long.

TIPS FOR ATTRACTING

- **The White-breasted Nuthatch is a common backyard visitor often seen walking upside down on trunks or branches of trees caching sunflower seeds or other foods it has taken from feeders.**
- **Providing feeders without perches gives the advantage to nuthatches, woodpeckers, and chickadees to use those feeders more exclusively.**
- **Spreading peanut butter or soft suet directly on the rough bark of trees will provide a special treat for the nuthatches and other birds that can cling to tree bark.**

IN YOUR YARD

The White-breasted Nuthatch will be a year-long visitor within its range, so once you attract them to your yard, you will be seeing quite a bit of them. They are not a constant visitor; they will feed, cache some seeds, leave for some time, and then revisit. Both White-breasted Nuthatches and Red-breasted Nuthatches are vocal, and you will quickly learn their nasally calls when they are nearby. They are infrequent nest box users but may use them if the dimensions specified earlier are used in the construction of the nest box.

White-crowned Sparrow
Zonotrichia leucophrys

Male and female White-crowned Sparrows are identical in appearance.

GENERAL INFORMATION

- **Male:** A small gray-breasted sparrow with black-and-white stripes on upper part of head.
- **Female:** The female White-crowned Sparrow is not visibly different from the male.
- **Range:** Found throughout the US.
- **Migration:** Winters in the lower two-thirds of the US, migrates through the upper one-third, with some breeding and year-round residence in the Northwest.
- **Preferred Food:** Cracked corn, millet, sunflower seed.
- **Preferred Feeders:** Ground forager.
- **Nesting:**
  - **Natural:** A cuplike nest made from twigs and needles, lined with finer natural materials.
  - **Man-made:** Will not nest in man-made structures.

- **Eggs:** Creamy green with heavy splotching, approximately ⅞" long.

TIPS FOR ATTRACTING

- **The White-crowned Sparrow is very much a ground feeder and will pick at seed that has been dropped by other birds at the feeders.**
- **Like many sparrows, the White-crowned Sparrow will use a brush pile if one is available, so consider placing tree trimmings on the side for this species and many others.**
- **For those in the cold winter range of the White-crowned Sparrow, consider a heated birdbath to provide an ice-free water source for drinking.**

IN YOUR YARD

For many in the US, this species will either be a winter resident or a seasonal migrant. They have a specific strategy for finding food called "double scratching." This involves their hopping backward in place twice to remove leaves and litter from the ground in order to find seeds or small invertebrates to eat. They are timid and may be scared off by other larger birds coming into the feeding station area, but they will return when things quiet down.

White-throated Sparrow
Zonotrichia albicollis

Male and female White-throated Sparrows are identical in appearance.

GENERAL INFORMATION

- **Male:** A small gray-breasted sparrow with white throat and eye stripe and yellow between bill and eye.
- **Female:** The female White-throated Sparrow is not visibly different from the male.
- **Range:** Found east of the Rockies.
- **Migration:** Winters in the Ohio River Valley and southward into Texas, migrates through the Plains states, some year-round residence in New England.
- **Preferred Food:** Cracked corn, millet, sunflower seed.
- **Preferred Feeders:** Ground forager.
- **Nesting:**
  - **Natural:** A nest made in a depression in the ground, lined with fine natural materials in an area with dense ground cover.
  - **Man-made:** Will not nest in man-made structures.

- **Eggs:** Creamy green with heavy splotching, approximately ⅞" long.

TIPS FOR ATTRACTING

- **The White-throated Sparrow is similar in behavior to the White-crowned Sparrow in that it is exclusively a ground forager looking for seed spilled by other backyard visitors.**
- **The breeding area for White-throated Sparrows is the forest, which may explain why it enjoys hiding near thickets, hedges, and brush piles if available in your backyard.**
- **If you live in the winter range of this species, consider having a heated birdbath in winter when temperatures drop below freezing.**

IN YOUR YARD

The White-throated Sparrow's song "Old Sam Peabody, Peabody, Peabody" is instantly recognizable. As with the White-crowned Sparrow, the White-throated Sparrow will be a seasonal visitor either in winter or spring and during fall migration. Enjoy this sparrow and its song while you can.

Yellow-rumped Warbler
Setophaga coronata

Male and female

GENERAL INFORMATION

- **Male:** A small blue-gray-backed bird with white belly and yellow on crown, sides, and rump.
- **Female:** The female is similar to the male with muted yellow coloring, and is grayish instead of blue-gray.
- **Range:** Found in the Rockies and states eastward.
- **Migration:** Breeds in the Rockies and New England, migrates through the central plains, and winters in the southern two-thirds of the US from Texas eastward.
- **Preferred Food:** Mealworms, suet.
- **Preferred Feeders:** Suet feeder, wire mesh (mealworms).
- **Nesting:**

- **Natural:** A cuplike nest made from twigs and needles, lined with animal hair and built on the branch of a conifer tree.
- **Man-made:** Will not nest in man-made structures.
- **Eggs:** Creamy with brown splotching, approximately ¾" long.

TIPS FOR ATTRACTING

- **Although they are insect eaters, Yellow-rumped Warblers will come to feeders for suet and mealworms, plus peanut butter and sunflower seed on occasion.**
- **In winter, Yellow-rumped Warblers will feed on berries from juniper and dogwood, plus grapes either cultivated or wild if planted in your yard.**
- **Many species of warblers are attracted to backyards not for food but for dynamic water sources, such as drippers, misters, or water agitators.**

IN YOUR YARD

Unless you live in the Yellow-rumped Warbler's breeding area, you will see them in winter or during spring and fall migration when they are fairly common. They are very active foragers in trees, so be sure to check out the upper branches of your trees for movement when they are in your area.

Printed in Great Britain
by Amazon